EDITOR: Maryanne Blacker
FOOD EDITOR: Pamela Clark

• • •

DESIGNER: Robbylee Phelan
ARTIST: Jennifer Rudd

• • •

DEPUTY FOOD EDITOR: Jan Castorina
ASSISTANT FOOD EDITOR: Kathy Snowball
ASSOCIATE FOOD EDITOR: Enid Morrison
SENIOR HOME ECONOMISTS: Alexandra McCowan,
Louise Patniotis, Kathy Wharton
HOME ECONOMISTS: Cynthia Black, Leisel Chen,
Kathy McGarry, Tracey Port, Maggie Quickenden,
Dimitra Stais
EDITORIAL COORDINATOR: Elizabeth Hooper
KITCHEN ASSISTANT: Amy Wong

• • •

STYLISTS: Lucy Andrews, Marie-Helene Clauzon,
Carolyn Fienberg, Jane Hann, Rosemary de Santis

PHOTOGRAPHERS: Kevin Brown, Robert Clark,
Robert Taylor, Jon Waddy

• • •

HOME LIBRARY STAFF:

ASSISTANT EDITOR: Beverley Hudec
ART DIRECTOR: Paula Wooller
EDITORIAL COORDINATOR: Fiona Nicholas

• • •

PUBLISHER: Richard Walsh
ASSOCIATE PUBLISHER: Bob Neil

• • •

Produced by The Australian Women's Weekly Home Library.
Typeset by ACP Colour Graphics Pty Ltd. Printed by Dai
Nippon Co., Ltd in Japan.
Published by ACP Publishing Pty Ltd, 54 Park Street, Sydney.
♦ AUSTRALIA: Distributed by Network Distribution Company,
54 Park Street Sydney, (02) 282 8777.
♦ UNITED KINGDOM: Distributed in the U.K. by Australian
Consolidated Press (UK) Ltd, 20 Galowhill Rd, Brackmills,
Northampton NN4 OEE (0604) 760 456.
♦ CANADA: Distributed in Canada by Whitecap
Books Ltd, 1086 West 3rd St,
North Vancouver V7P 3J6 (604) 980 9852.
♦ NEW ZEALAND: Distributed in New Zealand by Netlink
Distribution Company, 17B Hargreaves St, Level 5,
College Hill, Auckland 1 (9) 302 7616.
♦ SOUTH AFRICA: Distributed in South Africa by Intermag,
PO Box 57394, Springfield 2137 (011) 493 3200.
ACN 053 273 546

• • •

Salads

Includes index.
ISBN 0 949128 96 1.

1.Salads. (Series: Australian Women's
Weekly Home Library).

641.83

• • •

COVER: Best Caesar Salad, page 108
Plate: NSW Craft Centre, The Rocks. Bowl: Made Where.
OPPOSITE: Pickled Vegetables with
Deep-Fried Bocconcini, page 66.
BACK COVER: Open Herb Ravioli with Prawns and
Pesto, page 45.

Salads

From over 200 recipes you can choose sensational, fresh salads with flavour influences from around the world. They range from the most basic to the very unusual, and there is something for every occasion from a barbecue to a formal sit-down meal. We've used readily available ingredients, plus lots of pretty leaves; the more unusual ones are pictured in our glossary. And if you're wondering how to choose a salad, why not start with the season? Find out what fresh produce is best at the time, and then select a method for serving it from among the delicious recipes featured in our book. Even your own garden can provide lettuce, herbs or tomatoes, or you could think of growing some in pots if you don't have a garden.

Pamela Clark

FOOD EDITOR

BRITISH & NORTH AMERICAN READERS: Please note that Australian cup and spoon measurements are metric. A quick conversion guide appears on page 127.
A glossary explaining unfamiliar terms and ingredients appears on page 121.

MAIN COURSES

Some salads in this section are hearty, some are light, and all are satisfying, delicious and as stylish or as simple as the occasion requires. We've made a tempting range based on beef, lamb, pork and veal, poultry, seafood, eggs and cheese, plus some recipes without meat, giving a choice for everyone. Where suitable, some recipes would be equally good as an entree if served in smaller portions; others could double as light lunches and snacks. Indeed, for most recipes you'll find it easy to adjust the quantities up or down depending on how many you are serving – and their appetites. Most dressings can be made a day ahead; salads are best made just before serving.

NUTTY BEEF AND ASPARAGUS SALAD

2 bunches (about 500g) fresh
    asparagus spears
2 tablespoons olive oil
750g sliced beef rump steak
160g snow pea sprouts
1 cup (100g) pecans or walnuts

TARRAGON DRESSING
2 tablespoons chopped fresh tarragon
2 tablespoons lemon juice
½ cup (125ml) olive oil
1 teaspoon honey
1 teaspoon French mustard

Boil, steam or microwave asparagus until just tender; drain, rinse under cold water, drain. Heat oil in pan, add steak in batches, cook until browned and done as desired; cool. Slice steak thinly. Combine asparagus, steak, sprouts and nuts in bowl; drizzle with tarragon dressing.
Tarragon Dressing: Combine all ingredients in screw-top jar; shake well.
Serves 4.

MEATBALL AND MANGO SALAD

Meatballs suitable to freeze.

1kg minced beef
1 tablespoon chopped fresh coriander
2 cloves garlic, crushed
2 green shallots, chopped
¾ cup (180ml) coconut milk
1 cup (70g) stale breadcrumbs
2 cups (140g) shredded coconut
2 medium mangoes
2 green shallots, extra

DRESSING
½ cup (125ml) oil
½ cup (125ml) cider vinegar
2 small fresh red chillies,
    finely chopped
1 tablespoon brown sugar
3 teaspoons chopped fresh coriander

Combine mince, coriander, garlic, chopped shallots, milk and breadcrumbs in bowl; mix well. Roll 2 level teaspoons of mixture into balls, roll in coconut. Place meatballs in single layer on greased oven tray. Bake, uncovered, in moderately hot oven about 20 minutes or until cooked through, drain; cool.

Cut 1½ of the mangoes into 1cm x 6cm strips. Reserve remaining mango for dressing. Cut extra shallots into 6cm thin strips. Combine meatballs, mango strips and extra shallot strips in large bowl; drizzle with dressing.
Dressing: Chop remaining mango finely, combine with remaining ingredients in screw-top jar; shake well.
Serves 4.

RIGHT: From back: Nutty Beef and Asparagus Salad, Meatball and Mango Salad.

Plates from Amy's Tableware; tiles from Pazotti.

PASTRAMI WITH ROASTED TOMATO AND ONION SALAD

1 tablespoon olive oil
10 (about 250g) baby onions
250g cherry tomatoes, halved
1/4 cup (60ml) olive oil, extra
1 tablespoon chopped fresh
   lemon thyme
1 tablespoon chopped fresh oregano
1 tablespoon chopped fresh basil
2 cloves garlic, crushed
12 drained artichoke hearts
2 cups (300g) frozen broad beans
2 bunches (about 240g) rocket
1 medium radicchio lettuce
1 medium red oak leaf lettuce
350g sliced pastrami

DRESSING
1/2 teaspoon cracked black
   peppercorns
2 tablespoons lemon juice

Heat oil in pan, add whole onions, cook, stirring, until browned. Transfer onions to baking dish, bake, uncovered, in moderate oven 10 minutes; remove from dish.

Place tomatoes, cut side up, in baking dish, sprinkle with extra oil, herbs and garlic. Bake, uncovered, in moderate oven about 5 minutes or until tomatoes are warm. Remove tomatoes from dish, reserve oil for dressing.

Cut artichokes into quarters. Pour boiling water over beans in heatproof bowl, drain immediately; peel.

Combine onions, tomatoes, artichokes, beans, rocket, torn lettuce and pastrami on plates; drizzle with dressing.
Dressing: Combine reserved oil mixture with remaining ingredients in screw-top jar; shake well.

Serves 4.

BEEF, BOK CHOY AND BLACK BEAN SALAD

Beef can be marinated a day ahead; store, covered, in refrigerator.

600g piece beef eye-fillet
2 tablespoons oil
1 lime
2 teaspoons sesame oil
1 tablespoon oil, extra
3 cloves garlic, crushed
1 teaspoon grated fresh ginger
1 bunch (about 600g) bok
   choy, chopped
2 teaspoons lime juice
2 teaspoons salted black
   beans, rinsed
1 1/2 tablespoons black bean sauce
2 tablespoons raw peanuts

MARINADE
2 tablespoons salted black
   beans, rinsed
1/4 cup (60ml) dry sherry
1/4 cup (60ml) light soy sauce
1 tablespoon honey
1 green shallot, chopped
1/4 teaspoon sambal oelek
1/4 teaspoon five spice powder
1 teaspoon grated fresh ginger

Pour marinade over beef in bowl, cover, refrigerate several hours or overnight.

Remove beef from marinade; reserve marinade. Heat oil in pan, add beef, cook over high heat until well browned all over. Transfer beef to baking dish, bake, uncovered, in very hot oven about 10 minutes or until cooked as desired, brushing occasionally with reserved marinade. Stand beef 5 minutes before slicing.

Using a vegetable peeler, peel rind from lime; cut rind into thin strips.

Heat sesame oil and extra oil in wok, add garlic and ginger, stir-fry until aromatic. Add bok choy, stir-fry 2 minutes. Add rind, juice, black beans, sauce and peanuts to wok, stir-fry until combined.

Place bok choy mixture on plate, top with sliced beef. Serve warm or cold.
Marinade: Blend or process black beans and sherry until smooth, add remaining ingredients, blend until combined.

Serves 4.

ITALIAN MEATBALL SALAD WITH PESTO WEDGES

Meatballs suitable to freeze.

2 pitta pocket breads
1/3 cup (80ml) mayonnaise
1 tablespoon milk
1 cup (220g) risoni pasta
2 tablespoons olive oil
1 tablespoon lemon juice
1/4 cup shredded fresh basil
2 tablespoons chopped fresh chives
2/3 cup (70g) drained sun-dried
   tomatoes, sliced
150g mozzarella cheese, chopped
1 cup (150g) pimiento-stuffed green
   olives, halved

PESTO
1 cup firmly packed fresh basil leaves
1 clove garlic, crushed
2 tablespoons pine nuts, toasted
1/2 cup (125ml) olive oil

MEATBALLS
500g minced beef
1 cup (70g) stale breadcrumbs
2 cloves garlic, crushed
1 medium onion, grated
1 egg, lightly beaten
oil for deep-frying

Split pitta breads in half, cut into wedges. Brush half the pesto mixture onto split side of bread. Place bread, split side up, on oven tray. Bake in moderate oven about 15 minutes or until bread is crisp; cool.

Combine remaining pesto mixture, mayonnaise and milk in bowl; mix well.

Add pasta to pan of boiling water, boil, uncovered, until just tender; drain, rinse under cold water, drain well. Combine pasta, oil, juice, herbs, tomatoes, cheese, olives and meatballs in bowl; drizzle with pesto mayonnaise mixture. Serve with pesto wedges.
Pesto: Blend or process all ingredients until smooth.
Meatballs: Combine mince, breadcrumbs, garlic, onion and egg in bowl; mix well. Roll 2 level teaspoons of mixture into balls. Deep-fry meatballs in hot oil until browned, drain on absorbent paper; cool.

Serves 4.

LEFT: Clockwise from top left: Beef, Bok Choy and Black Bean Salad, Italian Meatball Salad with Pesto Wedges, Pastrami with Roasted Tomato and Onion Salad.

Tiles from Pazotti.

MINCED BEEF WITH EGG AND SHALLOT SALAD

1 tablespoon oil
2 tablespoons sesame oil
1 medium onion, finely chopped
2 small fresh red chillies,
    finely chopped
4 cloves garlic, crushed
2 teaspoons grated lime rind
1/3 cup (50g) raw peanuts, chopped
2 tablespoons dried shrimp
1/2 teaspoon ground cardamom
1/2 teaspoon ground cumin
500g minced beef
3 teaspoons fish sauce
2 tablespoons lime juice
2 tablespoons chopped
    fresh coriander

EGG AND SHALLOT SALAD
2 green shallots
2 teaspoons sesame oil
2 teaspoons sweet sherry
2 teaspoons fish sauce
2 teaspoons lime juice
1/2 teaspoon honey
8 eggs
1 tablespoon grated fresh ginger

Heat both oils in pan, add onion, chillies, garlic, rind, peanuts, shrimp and spices, cook, stirring, until onion is soft. Add mince, cook, stirring, until mince is browned. Stir in sauce, juice and coriander; cool. Serve mince mixture with egg and shallot salad.

Egg and Shallot Salad: Cut shallots into 5cm thin strips. Combine shallots, oil, sherry, sauce, juice and honey in bowl.

Whisk eggs and ginger together in another bowl. Pour enough egg mixture to cover base of heated greased pan, cook until lightly browned underneath, turn omelette, brown other side. Repeat with remaining mixture. Finely shred omelettes, add to shallot mixture; mix well.

Serves 4.

BELOW: From left: Beef and Three Pepper Salad, Minced Beef with Egg and Shallot Salad.

Plates, spoons and bamboo blind from Made in Japan Imports.

BEEF AND THREE PEPPER SALAD

600g piece beef rump steak
2 teaspoons seasoned pepper
1 tablespoon olive oil
2 medium green peppers
2 medium red peppers
2 medium yellow peppers
3 green shallots, sliced
1 small bunch curly endive

VINAIGRETTE
¼ cup (60ml) olive oil
1 tablespoon lemon juice
2 teaspoons white wine vinegar
½ teaspoon sugar
½ teaspoon chopped fresh thyme
1 clove garlic, crushed

Sprinkle both sides of steak with seasoned pepper. Heat oil in pan, add steak, cook until done as desired. Remove steak from pan; cool.

Cut steak into thin slices. Quarter peppers, remove seeds and membranes. Grill peppers, skin side up, until skin blisters and blackens. Peel away skin, cut peppers into thin strips. Combine steak, pepper strips, shallots and vinaigrette in bowl; mix well. Serve beef and three pepper salad with curly endive.

Vinaigrette: Combine all ingredients in screw-top jar; shake well.

Serves 4.

JAPANESE-STYLE BEEF SALAD

2 tablespoons oil
8 (about 1kg) beef fillet steaks
½ cup (100g) short-grain rice
½ x 13g packet nori seaweed
2 medium carrots
2 sticks celery
½ large (about 200g) daikon
4 radishes, coarsely grated
50g packet pickled pink ginger, finely shredded

SOY AND SESAME SAUCE
1 tablespoon soy sauce
1 tablespoon mirin
1 teaspoon sesame seeds
½ teaspoon sugar
¼ teaspoon sesame oil

WASABI SAUCE
2 teaspoons wasabi paste
1 tablespoon mirin
1 tablespoon water

Heat oil in pan, add steaks, cook until well browned and done as desired; remove from pan, cool.

Slice steaks thinly. Add rice gradually to pan of boiling water, boil, uncovered, until tender; drain, rinse under cold water, cool.

Place seaweed in bowl, cover with cold water, stand briefly until softened; drain, pat dry with absorbent paper. Shred seaweed finely.

Cut carrots, celery and daikon into long, thin strips. Place all ingredients separately on individual plates; top rice with seaweed shreds. Serve salad with soy and sesame sauce and wasabi sauce.

Soy and Sesame Sauce: Combine all ingredients in screw-top jar; shake well.

Wasabi Sauce: Blend paste, mirin and water in bowl; mix well.

Serves 4.

ABOVE: Japanese-Style Beef Salad.

Red tray, black tray, chopsticks and white sauce dishes from Made in Japan Imports.

7

BARBECUED BEEF AND BEETROOT SALAD

6 medium beetroot
3 medium oranges
2 tablespoons chopped fresh tarragon
1 medium green pepper, finely sliced
2 green shallots, chopped
1.2kg piece beef eye-fillet, thinly sliced
2 medium green oak leaf lettuces

DRESSING
1 cup (250ml) orange juice
1½ tablespoons tarragon vinegar
2 teaspoons prepared horseradish
¼ teaspoon sugar
2 tablespoons chopped fresh tarragon
1 clove garlic, crushed
½ teaspoon French mustard
¾ cup (180ml) olive oil

Cut leaves from beetroot, reserve 12 leaves. Grate beetroot.

Using vegetable peeler, peel rind thinly from oranges, cut rind into thin strips.

Combine beetroot, rind, tarragon and 1¼ cups (310ml) of the dressing in bowl, cover, stand 2 hours. Just before serving add pepper and shallots; mix well.

Grill or barbecue beef slices until cooked as desired.

Toss reserved beetroot leaves and torn lettuce leaves in remaining dressing, top with beetroot salad and beef.

Dressing: Combine all ingredients in screw-top jar; shake well.

Serves 6.

BEEF AND VEGETABLE SHELLS WITH GINGER DRESSING

Steak can be marinated a day ahead; store, covered, in refrigerator.

500g beef rump steak, thinly sliced
1 tablespoon oil
2 medium carrots
1 medium red pepper
1 medium yellow pepper
2 medium zucchini
2 sticks celery
1 tablespoon oil, extra
1 clove garlic, crushed
1 tablespoon light soy sauce
20 extra large pasta shells

MARINADE
2 tablespoons light soy sauce
1 tablespoon sesame oil
1 tablespoon honey
1 tablespoon brown sugar
1 teaspoon five spice powder
2 cloves garlic, crushed
1 tablespoon grated fresh ginger
2 tablespoons sweet sherry

DRESSING
1 tablespoon soy sauce
2 tablespoons sesame oil
2 tablespoons brown sugar
1 tablespoon grated fresh ginger

Combine steak with marinade in bowl, cover, refrigerate several hours or overnight. Drain steak from marinade, discard marinade. Heat oil in pan, cook steak in batches until well browned and tender; drain on absorbent paper.

Cut carrots, peppers, zucchini and celery into thin strips. Heat extra oil in pan, add vegetables and garlic, stir-fry until just tender, stir in sauce; cool. Combine steak and vegetable mixture in bowl.

Add pasta to large pan of boiling water, boil, uncovered, until just tender; drain. Spoon the steak and vegetable mixture into each pasta shell; drizzle with dressing.
Marinade: Combine all ingredients in bowl; mix well.
Dressing: Combine all ingredients in screw-top jar; shake well.

Serves 4.

RED CABBAGE, SAUSAGE AND CORIANDER SALAD

8 (about 700g) thick beef sausages
250g spaghetti pasta
½ small red cabbage, shredded
8 green shallots, chopped
12 fresh dates, pitted, sliced

DRESSING
⅓ cup chopped fresh coriander
1 tablespoon chopped fresh basil
1 tablespoon grated parmesan cheese
⅓ cup (80ml) olive oil
2 tablespoons lime juice
1 clove garlic, crushed
½ teaspoon sambal oelek

Cook sausages in pan until browned and cooked through; drain on absorbent paper, cool. Slice sausages thinly.

Add pasta to large pan of boiling water, boil, uncovered, until just tender; drain, rinse under cold water, drain well.

Combine sausages, pasta, cabbage, shallots, dates and dressing in bowl, cover, refrigerate 1 hour.
Dressing: Blend or process all ingredients until smooth.

Serves 4.

HOT STEAK AND CRUNCHY POTATO SALAD

600g beef fillet steak
2 teaspoons seasoned pepper
2 teaspoons garlic salt
1 tablespoon oil
1 medium cos lettuce
1 bunch (about 650g) English spinach, shredded
2 cups (about 100g) firmly packed watercress sprigs
2 small avocados, sliced

CRUNCHY POTATOES
2 medium potatoes
1 tablespoon oil
20g butter

CREAMY DRESSING
2 teaspoons seeded mustard
2 teaspoons horseradish cream
1 teaspoon brown sugar
⅓ cup (80ml) olive oil
1½ tablespoons white wine vinegar
⅓ cup (80ml) cream

Cut steak into 1cm strips. Combine steak, pepper and salt in bowl. Heat oil in pan, add steak, cook in batches until browned and tender; drain on absorbent paper.

Combine torn lettuce leaves, spinach and watercress in bowl, top with avocados, hot steak and crunchy potatoes; drizzle with creamy dressing.
Crunchy Potatoes: Peel potatoes, cut into 1½cm cubes. Heat oil and butter in baking dish, add potatoes, stir to coat in oil mixture. Bake, uncovered, in hot oven about 35 minutes or until crisp, turning occasionally; drain on absorbent paper.
Creamy Dressing: Combine all ingredients in pan, whisk over heat until warm.

Serves 4.

LEFT: Clockwise from back: Red Cabbage, Sausage and Coriander Salad, Beef and Vegetable Shells with Ginger Dressing, Barbecued Beef and Beetroot Salad. ABOVE: Hot Steak and Crunchy Potato Salad.

Left: White plates and salad servers from Hale Imports; glass plates and checked cloth from Accoutrement.
Above: Plate from Mura Clay Gallery.

BEEF AND BEAN SALAD WITH RED PEPPER MAYONNAISE

1.2kg beef sirloin
1 tablespoon olive oil
1 bunch (about 250g) snake beans
250g cherry tomatoes
250g yellow tear drop tomatoes
1 cup (about 180g) baby black olives
⅓ cup shredded fresh basil
2 tablespoons chopped fresh chives
2 tablespoons chopped fresh parsley

DRESSING
1 clove garlic, crushed
1½ tablespoons balsamic vinegar
½ cup (125ml) virgin olive oil

RED PEPPER MAYONNAISE
1 large red pepper
1 egg yolk
½ teaspoon French mustard
1 teaspoon white wine vinegar
¼ cup (60ml) olive oil
¼ cup (60ml) grapeseed oil

Tie beef with string at 4cm intervals. Heat oil in pan, add beef, cook until well browned all over. Transfer beef to wire rack in baking dish, bake, uncovered, in moderately hot oven about 25 minutes or until cooked as desired; cool.

Cut beans into 10cm lengths. Boil, steam or microwave beans until just tender; drain, rinse under cold water, drain. Combine beans, tomatoes, olives, herbs and dressing in bowl; mix well. Serve bean salad with sliced beef and red pepper mayonnaise.
Dressing: Combine all ingredients in screw-top jar; shake well.
Red Pepper Mayonnaise: Quarter pepper, remove seeds and membrane. Grill pepper, skin side up, until skin blisters and blackens; peel skin. Blend or process pepper until smooth, push through sieve. Blend or process egg yolk, mustard and vinegar until smooth. With motor operating gradually pour in combined oils in a thin stream, blend until thickened. Add pepper puree, blend until smooth.
Serves 6.

THAI-STYLE BEEF SALAD

1 medium red pepper
1 tablespoon oil
600g piece beef rump steak
25g rice vermicelli noodles
oil for deep-frying
1 small cos lettuce
1 small radicchio lettuce
2 medium tomatoes, peeled, seeded, chopped
2 green shallots, chopped

DRESSING
⅓ cup (80ml) lime juice
¼ cup (60ml) fish sauce
1 tablespoon chopped fresh lemon grass
1 tablespoon chopped fresh mint
1 tablespoon chopped fresh coriander
1 tablespoon honey
1 clove garlic, crushed
2 small fresh red chillies, finely chopped

Quarter pepper, remove seeds and membrane. Grill pepper, skin side up, until skin blisters and blackens. Peel skin, cut pepper into strips. Heat oil in pan, add steak, cook until well browned and done as desired. Remove steak from pan; cool.

Cut steak into thin slices. Combine steak and 2 tablespoons of the dressing in bowl; mix well.

Deep-fry noodles in batches in hot oil about 5 seconds or until puffed and white; drain on absorbent paper.

Combine pepper, torn lettuce leaves, tomatoes, shallots and remaining dressing in bowl; mix well. Place lettuce mixture on plates, top mixture with steak then crisp noodles.
Dressing: Combine all ingredients in screw-top jar; shake well.
Serves 4.

BEEF SALAD CUPS WITH TOMATO SALSA

1 tablespoon oil
2 large onions, finely chopped
500g minced beef
2 cloves garlic, crushed
1 teaspoon beef stock powder
1 medium witlof
¼ cup (20g) parmesan cheese flakes

TOMATO SALSA
250g cherry tomatoes, quartered
6 green shallots, chopped
2 tablespoons olive oil
1 tablespoon lemon juice

Heat oil in pan, add onions, cook, stirring, until soft, add mince, garlic and stock powder, cook, stirring, until mince is browned and mixture dry. Transfer mixture to bowl, cool.

Cover mince mixture, refrigerate until cold. Separate witlof leaves. Spoon mince mixture into leaves, serve topped with tomato salsa and cheese.
Tomato Salsa: Combine all ingredients in bowl; cover, refrigerate 1 hour.
Serves 4.

ABOVE: Thai-Style Beef Salad.
RIGHT: From left: Beef and Bean Salad with Red Pepper Mayonnaise, Beef Salad Cups with Tomato Salsa.

Above: Plate from Amy's Tableware; tiles from Pazotti.

Right: Plates from Hale Imports; coasters and salad servers from Made in Japan Imports.

CREAMY LAMB AND SWISS CHEESE SALAD

1 tablespoon oil
4 (about 600g) lamb steaks
200g Swiss cheese, sliced
10 dill pickle gherkins, sliced
250g cherry tomatoes, halved
4 green shallots, chopped
6 cos lettuce leaves
6 butter lettuce leaves

DRESSING
2 teaspoons chopped fresh dill
1 cup (250ml) light sour cream
1 tablespoon seeded mustard
1 tablespoon horseradish cream
1 teaspoon cracked
  black peppercorns

Heat oil in pan, add lamb, cook until browned and tender; drain, cool. Cut lamb into thin strips. Cut cheese into thin strips. Combine lamb, cheese, gherkins, tomatoes, shallots and torn lettuce leaves in bowl, add dressing; mix well.
Dressing: Combine all ingredients in bowl; mix well.

Serves 4 to 6.

LAMB FILLET SALAD WITH SPICED CHICK PEAS

Chick peas are best prepared a day ahead; keep, covered, at room temperature. If you prefer, use 2 x 310g cans chick peas; drain and rinse before using.

1 cup (210g) dried chick peas
1 teaspoon ground cumin
1 teaspoon ground coriander
1 tablespoon curry powder
¼ teaspoon chilli powder
2 tablespoons oil
1 tablespoon oil, extra
6 (about 500g) lamb fillets

SALAD
1 cup firmly packed flat-leafed
  parsley, chopped
⅓ cup chopped fresh mint
1 clove garlic, crushed
2 medium tomatoes, peeled,
  seeded, chopped
1 small green cucumber, chopped

TOMATO CUMIN DRESSING
2 teaspoons cumin seeds
425g can tomatoes
¼ cup (60ml) olive oil
1 tablespoon white vinegar
1 tablespoon balsamic vinegar
1 teaspoon seasoned pepper

Place peas in large bowl, cover well with water, cover, stand overnight.
  Drain peas, rinse well. Add peas to pan of boiling water, simmer, uncovered, about 30 minutes or until tender; drain. Toss peas in combined spices and oil, spread in single layer on oven tray, bake, uncovered, in moderately hot oven about 45 minutes or until peas are lightly browned and crisp.
  Heat extra oil in pan, add lamb in batches, cook until tender; drain, cool. Slice lamb thinly. Top salad with peas and lamb; drizzle with tomato cumin dressing.
Salad: Combine all ingredients in bowl; mix well.
Tomato Cumin Dressing: Add cumin seeds to dry pan, stir over heat until fragrant. Blend or process undrained tomatoes until smooth; strain, discard seeds. Combine cumin seeds, strained puree, oil, both vinegars and pepper in screw-top jar; shake well.

Serves 4.

BARBECUED LAMB CUTLETS WITH POLENTA

12 lamb cutlets
1 large radicchio lettuce
1 large fennel bulb, thinly sliced
½ cup (55g) drained sun-dried
  tomatoes, sliced
½ cup (80g) black olives, pitted, sliced
½ cup shredded fresh basil
1 cup firmly packed flat-leafed parsley
½ cup (40g) parmesan cheese flakes

DRESSING
2 tablespoons balsamic vinegar
2 cloves garlic, crushed
1 tablespoon tomato paste
1 tablespoon water
⅔ cup (160ml) virgin olive oil

POLENTA
2½ cups (625ml) chicken stock
1½ cups (100g) polenta
¼ cup (20g) grated parmesan cheese
1 egg yolk
1 tablespoon chopped fresh rosemary
oil for deep-frying

Barbecue or grill lamb until tender. Combine lettuce leaves, fennel, tomatoes, olives, basil, parsley and cheese in bowl, add half the dressing; mix gently. Drizzle lamb with remaining dressing; serve with salad and polenta.
Dressing: Combine all ingredients in screw-top jar; shake well.
Polenta: Grease 8cm x 26cm bar pan, line base with paper, grease paper. Place stock in pan, bring to boil, add polenta, cook, stirring, about 7 minutes or until mixture is thick; cool 3 minutes. Stir in cheese, egg yolk and rosemary. Press mixture into prepared pan, cover, refrigerate 2 hours. Turn polenta out of pan, cut into 16 triangles. Deep-fry polenta in hot oil until browned; drain on absorbent paper.

Serves 4 to 6.

LEFT: Clockwise from top left: Barbecued Lamb Cutlets with Polenta, Creamy Lamb and Swiss Cheese Salad, Lamb Fillet Salad with Spiced Chick Peas.

Tiles from Terra Australis.

LAMB FILLET SALAD WITH WILD RICE

Lamb can be marinated a day ahead; store, covered, in refrigerator.

4 (about 350g) lamb fillets
1 tablespoon oil
1 small onion, grated
1 small fresh green chilli, finely chopped
1 clove garlic, crushed
1 teaspoon white vinegar
1 tablespoon teriyaki sauce
1 tablespoon honey
⅔ cup (130g) wild rice
250g kumara
450g green beans

DRESSING
½ x 250g packet frozen spinach, thawed
2 tablespoons chopped fresh coriander
1 tablespoon lime juice
½ teaspoon sesame oil
2 teaspoons fish sauce
⅓ cup (80ml) buttermilk
¼ teaspoon sugar
¼ cup (60ml) water

Combine lamb, oil, onion, chilli, garlic, vinegar, sauce and honey in bowl, cover, refrigerate several hours or overnight.

Remove lamb from marinade, reserve marinade. Place lamb in baking dish, bake, uncovered, in hot oven about 10 minutes or until tender, brushing occasionally with reserved marinade. Cool lamb, slice thinly.

Add rice to pan of boiling water, boil, uncovered, about 40 minutes or until tender, drain.

Cut kumara into 1cm pieces. Cut beans into 5cm lengths. Boil, steam or microwave kumara and beans separately until tender; drain, rinse under cold water, drain well. Place rice, kumara, beans and lamb on plates; drizzle with dressing.

Dressing: Blend or process all ingredients until smooth, push through fine sieve; cover, refrigerate 30 minutes.

Serves 4.

TANDOORI LAMB WITH PINEAPPLE SALSA

Lamb can be marinated a day ahead; store, covered, in refrigerator. Marinated lamb suitable to freeze.

12 lamb cutlets
2 cups (500ml) plain yogurt
6 cloves garlic, crushed
1½ tablespoons grated fresh ginger
1½ tablespoons paprika
1 teaspoon garam masala
pinch ground saffron
1½ teaspoons ground cardamom
½ teaspoon chilli powder
1 teaspoon ground coriander
1 teaspoon grated lime rind
2 tablespoons lime juice

PINEAPPLE SALSA
½ small pineapple, finely chopped
1 small green cucumber, finely chopped
2 teaspoons chopped fresh coriander
1 tablespoon lime juice

Place lamb in large bowl, pour over combined remaining ingredients, cover, refrigerate several hours or overnight.

Remove lamb from marinade, reserve marinade. Grill or barbecue lamb until tender, brushing with reserved marinade during cooking; cool. Serve tandoori lamb with pineapple salsa.

Pineapple Salsa: Combine all ingredients in bowl; cover, stand 1 hour.

Serves 4.

ABOVE LEFT: Tandoori Lamb with Pineapple Salsa.
RIGHT: From back: Lamb Fillet Salad with Wild Rice, Herbed Lamb Sausages with Rosemary Pasta.

Above left: Platter from Villeroy & Boch; bamboo blind from Made in Japan Imports.
Right: Plates, glasses and cutlery from The Design Store.

HERBED LAMB SAUSAGES WITH ROSEMARY PASTA

2 cups (300g) plain flour
¼ cup chopped fresh rosemary
3 eggs
1 medium red pepper, thinly sliced

GARLIC DRESSING
2 egg yolks
2 tablespoons white wine vinegar
3 cloves garlic, crushed
2 teaspoons Dijon mustard
1⅓ cups (330ml) oil
2 tablespoons water

HERBED LAMB SAUSAGES
1kg shoulder of lamb, boned
30g butter
1 medium onion, finely chopped
2 teaspoons sambal oelek
2 cloves garlic, crushed
1 egg
1 cup (70g) stale breadcrumbs
2 tablespoons chopped fresh parsley
1 tablespoon chopped fresh thyme
2 teaspoons oil

Mix flour, rosemary and eggs in bowl or processor until mixture forms a ball, adding a little water, if necessary (mixture should be firm but not flaky). Knead dough on lightly floured surface until smooth.

If making pasta by hand, cover dough, stand 20 minutes. Roll on lightly floured surface until about 2mm thick.

If using pasta machine, cut dough in half, roll each half through thickest setting of machine, fold dough in half. Repeat rolling and folding dough, gradually decreasing setting on machine until dough is about 2mm thick.

Cut pasta into 2cm strips. Add pasta to large pan of boiling water, boil, uncovered, about 5 minutes or until just tender; drain, rinse under cold water, drain. Combine pasta, pepper, garlic dressing and herbed lamb sausages in bowl; mix gently.

Garlic Dressing: Place egg yolks, vinegar, garlic and mustard in bowl, whisk until smooth. Add oil gradually in a thin stream while whisking, whisk until thick; stir in water.

Herbed Lamb Sausages: Trim fat from lamb, chop lamb roughly. Heat butter in pan, add onion, sambal oelek and garlic, cook, stirring, until onion is soft, cool. Process lamb, onion mixture and egg until smooth. Transfer mixture to bowl, stir in breadcrumbs and herbs. Divide mixture into 4 portions.

Spoon 1 portion of mixture along centre of piece of plastic wrap. Fold plastic wrap around mixture, forming sausage shape about 3cm in diameter. Repeat with remaining mixture. Wrap each roll in foil, twist ends to seal.

Add rolls to large pan of simmering water, simmer, covered, 10 minutes. Remove rolls from water, stand 5 minutes before unwrapping. Heat oil in pan, add sausages, cook until lightly browned all over; drain on absorbent paper; cool. Cut sausages diagonally into thin slices.

Serves 6.

BAKED LAMB AND EGGPLANT WITH GARLIC MAYONNAISE

1.5kg leg of lamb
1 large eggplant
coarse cooking salt
¼ cup (60ml) olive oil
1 bunch (about 650g) English
**   spinach, shredded**
½ cup (80g) black olives,
**   pitted, quartered**
175g feta cheese, cubed
¼ cup (40g) pine nuts, toasted

GARLIC MAYONNAISE
1 egg yolk
1 whole egg
1 clove garlic, crushed
1 teaspoon Dijon mustard
2 tablespoons lemon juice
1 cup (250ml) oil
1 tablespoon chopped fresh parsley

Place lamb on wire rack in baking dish, bake, uncovered, in moderate oven about 1½ hours or until cooked as desired; cool.

Cut eggplant into 1cm cubes, sprinkle with salt, stand 20 minutes. Rinse eggplant under cold water, drain, pat dry with absorbent paper.

Place eggplant in single layer in baking dish, drizzle with oil. Bake, uncovered, in moderate oven about 30 minutes or until just tender, stirring occasionally; cool. Top spinach with sliced lamb, eggplant, olives, cheese and pine nuts; serve with garlic mayonnaise.

Garlic Mayonnaise: Combine egg yolk, egg, garlic, mustard and half the juice in blender, blend 1 minute.

With motor operating, add half the oil in a slow, steady stream. Add remaining juice, then continue pouring oil in a thin stream; blend until thick. Transfer mayonnaise to bowl, stir in parsley.

Serves 6.

MARINATED LAMB WITH NUTTY CITRUS SALAD

Lamb is best marinated a day ahead; store, covered, in refrigerator.

1 tablespoon olive oil
6 (about 500g) lamb fillets
¼ cup (60ml) orange juice
¼ cup (60ml) lemon juice
1 tablespoon balsamic vinegar
½ cup (125ml) olive oil, extra
1 teaspoon grated lemon rind
1 medium coral lettuce
4 medium oranges, segmented
2 medium grapefruit, segmented
⅔ cup (110g) blanched
**   almonds, toasted**
4 green shallots, chopped
1½ cups (about 75g) firmly packed
**   watercress sprigs**

Heat oil in pan, add lamb in batches, cook until tender, drain on absorbent paper.

Slice lamb. Combine lamb, juices, vinegar, extra oil and rind in bowl; cover, refrigerate several hours or overnight.

Drain lamb, reserve marinade. Combine lamb, torn lettuce leaves, citrus segments, nuts, shallots and watercress in bowl; drizzle with reserved marinade.

Serves 4.

LAMB AND POTATO SALAD WITH MINT DRESSING

1kg baby new potatoes
2 tablespoons olive oil
10 (about 850g) lamb fillets
2 tablespoons chopped fresh chives

MINT DRESSING
4 egg yolks
⅓ cup (80ml) lime juice
2 cloves garlic, crushed
¼ cup (60ml) grapeseed oil
½ cup (125ml) oil
1 cup chopped fresh mint

Boil, steam or microwave potatoes until tender; drain.

Heat oil in pan, add lamb in batches, cook until well browned and tender; drain on absorbent paper.

Slice lamb. Combine potatoes and lamb in bowl, add dressing; mix gently, sprinkle with chives. Serve warm or cold.

Mint Dressing: Blend or process egg yolks, juice and garlic until smooth. Add combined oils gradually in a thin stream while motor is operating. Add mint, blend until combined.

Serves 6.

LEFT: Baked Lamb and Eggplant with Garlic Mayonnaise.
RIGHT: From left: Lamb and Potato Salad with Mint Dressing, Marinated Lamb with Nutty Citrus Salad.

Left: Plate from Amy's Tableware; tiles from Pazotti.
Right: Bowls and dressing set from The Design Store; silver bowl and salad servers from Bibelot.

LAMB PROSCIUTTO WITH MARINATED MUSHROOMS

150g sliced lamb prosciutto
1 medium radicchio lettuce
½ bunch (about 325g) English
    spinach
1 cup (about 50g) firmly packed
    watercress leaves
½ cup (125ml) olive oil
2 tablespoons balsamic vinegar
½ cup firmly packed fresh purple
    basil leaves
oil for deep-frying

MARINATED MUSHROOMS
15g (about 10) dried
    Chinese mushrooms
80g Shitake mushrooms, chopped
150g oyster mushrooms, halved
300g baby mushrooms, quartered
2 cloves garlic, crushed
1 small red Spanish onion,
    finely chopped
3 teaspoons grated lemon rind
2 tablespoons chopped
    fresh rosemary
¼ cup chopped fresh parsley
½ cup (125ml) lemon juice
1¼ cups (310ml) olive oil

Cut lamb, lettuce and spinach into thin strips. Combine lamb, lettuce, spinach, watercress, oil and vinegar in bowl; mix well. Deep-fry basil leaves in hot oil about 30 seconds or until crisp. Top lamb mixture with marinated mushrooms, sprinkle with basil leaves.
Marinated Mushrooms: Place dried mushrooms in bowl, cover with boiling water, stand 20 minutes. Drain mushrooms, discard liquid and stems; slice mushrooms thinly. Combine all mushrooms and remaining ingredients in bowl, stand 2 hours, stirring occasionally.
Serves 4.

COUSCOUS TABBOULEH WITH LAMB MEATBALLS

Meatballs suitable to freeze.

1 cup (250ml) boiling water
1½ cups (260g) couscous
⅓ cup (80ml) olive oil
1 clove garlic, crushed
2 medium red peppers,
    finely chopped
1½ cups chopped fresh parsley
8 green shallots, chopped
¾ cup (60g) grated parmesan cheese

DRESSING
¼ cup (60ml) olive oil
1 tablespoon red wine vinegar
1 tablespoon lemon juice

LAMB MEATBALLS
500g minced lamb
1 large onion, grated
1 tablespoon chopped fresh sage
3 cloves garlic, crushed
1 tablespoon tomato paste
1 egg, lightly beaten
1½ cups (110g) stale breadcrumbs

Pour water over couscous in bowl, stir, stand until water is absorbed. Heat oil in pan, add garlic and couscous, cook, stirring, until well combined; cool. Combine couscous mixture, peppers, parsley, shallots, parmesan cheese and dressing in bowl; mix well. Stir in lamb meatballs.
Dressing: Combine all ingredients in screw-top jar; shake well.
Lamb Meatballs: Combine all ingredients in bowl, mix well, cover, refrigerate 30 minutes. Roll 2 level teaspoons of mixture into balls, place in single layer on lightly greased oven tray, bake, uncovered, in hot oven about 20 minutes or until browned and cooked through; cool.
Serves 4.

RIGHT: Clockwise from back: Couscous Tabbouleh with Lamb Meatballs, Lamb Prosciutto with Marinated Mushrooms, Lemon-Crusted Lamb with Tahini Dip.

Plates and glass from Accoutrement; bowl and spoons from The Design Store; tiles from Pazotti.

LEMON-CRUSTED LAMB WITH TAHINI DIP

2 tablespoons pine nuts
2 tablespoons rolled oats
2 tablespoons sesame seeds
**¾ cup (75g) packaged
  dry breadcrumbs**
1 teaspoon grated lemon rind
2 teaspoons honey
2 teaspoons chopped fresh thyme
2 tablespoons chopped fresh parsley
¼ cup (20g) grated parmesan cheese
1 egg yolk
10 (about 850g) lamb fillets
plain flour
1 egg, lightly beaten
1 tablespoon milk
¼ cup (60ml) oil
2 medium lemons
2 medium limes
2 bunches (about 240g) rocket
2 cups (about 80g) snow pea sprouts

DRESSING
1½ tablespoons lemon juice
¼ cup (60ml) olive oil

TAHINI DIP
⅓ cup (80ml) plain yogurt
1 tablespoon lemon juice
1½ tablespoons tahini paste

Process nuts, oats and sesame seeds until smooth; transfer mixture to bowl. Stir in crumbs, rind, honey, herbs, cheese and egg yolk; mix well. Toss lamb in flour, shake away excess flour. Dip lamb into combined egg and milk, toss in breadcrumb mixture, press crumbs on firmly; refrigerate 1 hour.

Heat oil in pan, add lamb in batches, cook until lightly browned. Transfer lamb to oven tray in single layer, bake, uncovered in moderately hot oven 5 minutes, drain on absorbent paper. Cut lamb into 1cm slices.

Using a vegetable peeler, peel rind thinly from lemons and limes, avoiding white pith; cut rind into thin strips. Add rind to pan of boiling water, boil 30 seconds; drain, rinse under cold water, drain. Combine rocket, sprouts and rind, top with lamb; drizzle with dressing. Serve with tahini dip.

Dressing: Combine all ingredients in screw-top jar; shake well.
Tahini Dip: Combine all ingredients in bowl; mix well.

Serves 6.

MINCED MEAT SALAD WITH EGGPLANT CRISPS

2 tablespoons olive oil
1 medium onion, finely chopped
4 cloves garlic, crushed
¼ cup (40g) pine nuts
350g minced pork and veal
¼ cup shredded fresh basil
⅔ cup (50g) grated parmesan cheese
1½ bunches (about 180g) rocket
¼ cup (20g) parmesan cheese flakes

EGGPLANT CRISPS
1 large eggplant, thinly sliced
oil for deep-frying

TOMATO VINAIGRETTE
3 medium tomatoes, chopped
1 tablespoon olive oil
2 teaspoons balsamic vinegar

Heat oil in pan, add onion, garlic and pine nuts, cook, stirring, until onion is soft. Add mince, cook, stirring, until mince is cooked; cool.

Stir in basil and grated cheese. Serve mince mixture on rocket leaves, top with eggplant crisps and cheese flakes; drizzle with tomato vinaigrette.

Eggplant Crisps: Deep-fry eggplant slices in batches in hot oil until browned and crisp; drain on absorbent paper.

Tomato Vinaigrette: Blend or process all ingredients until well combined. Push tomato mixture through sieve; discard pulp and seeds.

Serves 4.

MEXICAN-STYLE TACOS WITH ANCHOVY DRESSING

6 bacon rashers, chopped
¼ small cabbage, shredded
1 cup (about 50g) firmly packed
    watercress sprigs
1 teaspoon sambal oelek
3 medium radishes, grated
1 small red pepper, finely chopped
1 medium avocado, chopped
8 jumbo taco shells

ANCHOVY DRESSING
2 anchovy fillets
1 clove garlic, crushed
1 tablespoon white wine vinegar
¼ cup (60ml) olive oil
¼ cup (60ml) thickened cream
1 teaspoon chopped fresh oregano

Add bacon to dry pan, stir over heat until crisp; drain on absorbent paper. Combine bacon, cabbage, watercress, sambal oelek, radishes and pepper in bowl; mix well; gently stir in avocado. Crisp taco shells in oven, following directions on packet. Fill taco shells with bacon mixture; drizzle with anchovy dressing.

Anchovy Dressing: Blend or process anchovy fillets, garlic, vinegar, oil and cream until smooth; stir in oregano.

Serves 4.

WARM LENTIL AND SAUSAGE SALAD

1 tablespoon oil
5 smoky pork sausages
1¼ cups (250g) brown lentils
425g can tomatoes
1 teaspoon sugar
2¼ cups (560ml) water
2 cloves garlic, crushed
1 bay leaf
1 tablespoon oil, extra
1 medium onion, chopped
3 bacon rashers, chopped
1 medium red pepper, chopped
1 medium green pepper, chopped

Heat oil in pan, add sausages, cook until browned and tender; drain on absorbent paper. Cut into 1cm slices.

Combine lentils, undrained crushed tomatoes, sugar, water, garlic and bay leaf in pan, simmer, covered, about 35 minutes or until lentils are just tender and liquid is absorbed.

Heat extra oil in pan, add onion and bacon, cook, stirring, until onion is soft. Add sausages and peppers, cook, stirring, until sausages are heated through. Combine sausage mixture and lentil mixture in bowl; mix gently. Serve salad warm, or cold if desired.

Serves 4.

LEFT: Clockwise from left: Minced Meat Salad with Eggplant Crisps, Warm Lentil and Sausage Salad, Mexican-Style Tacos with Anchovy Dressing.

Plates from Mura Clay Gallery; tiles from Terra Australis.

SPICY SAUSAGE AND BEAN SALAD

1 cup (185g) dried black-eyed beans
3 cups (750ml) chicken stock
1 tablespoon olive oil
325g hot csabai sausage, sliced
1 medium onion, thinly sliced
1 medium red pepper, chopped
1 medium green pepper, chopped
1 large zucchini, chopped
½ cup (40g) parmesan cheese flakes
12 black olives, pitted, quartered
⅓ cup shredded fresh basil

DRESSING
2 medium tomatoes, chopped
¼ cup (60ml) oil
1 clove garlic, crushed
2 teaspoons red wine vinegar
½ teaspoon sugar

Place beans in bowl, cover well with water, cover, stand overnight.

Drain beans, combine with stock in pan, simmer, covered, about 25 minutes or until beans are just tender; drain, cool.

Heat oil in pan, add sausage and onion, cook, stirring, until sausage is slightly crisp; drain on absorbent paper, cool. Combine beans, sausage mixture, remaining ingredients and dressing in bowl; mix well.

Dressing: Blend or process tomatoes until smooth, strain. Combine tomato puree with remaining ingredients in screw-top jar; shake well.

Serves 4.

TORTELLINI SALAD WITH TOMATOES AND BASIL

1kg pork and veal tortellini
4 large tomatoes, peeled, seeded, chopped
1 medium red Spanish onion, chopped
1 cup (160g) black olives, pitted, sliced
¼ cup shredded fresh basil
2 tablespoons chopped fresh chives
2 cloves garlic, crushed
½ cup (125ml) olive oil
2 tablespoons white vinegar
¼ teaspoon freshly ground black pepper

Add tortellini to large pan of boiling water, boil, uncovered, until tender; drain, rinse under cold water, drain. Combine tortellini with remaining ingredients in bowl; mix well. Cover, refrigerate until cold.

Serves 4.

BELOW: Spicy Sausage and Bean Salad.
RIGHT: From left: Tortellini Salad with Tomatoes and Basil, Veal with Noodles and Bean Salad.

Below: Tiles from Country Floors.
Right: Plate and basket from Accoutrement.

VEAL WITH NOODLES AND BEAN SALAD

Veal can be marinated a day ahead; store, covered, in refrigerator.

500g veal fillet
½ cup (110g) dried adzuki beans
2 tablespoons oil
300g snake beans
500g thick egg noodles
2 teaspoons cornflour
½ cup (125ml) water
1 teaspoon sugar
1 tablespoon light soy sauce

MARINADE
1 medium orange
½ cup (125ml) orange juice
1 tablespoon grated fresh ginger
2 tablespoons honey
1 tablespoon Dijon mustard

Combine veal and marinade in bowl, cover, refrigerate several hours.

Cover adzuki beans with water in bowl, stand 3 hours. Drain adzuki beans, rinse well. Add adzuki beans to pan of water, bring to boil, simmer, uncovered, about 30 minutes or until tender; drain.

Remove veal from marinade, discard rind, reserve remaining marinade for sauce. Heat oil in baking dish, add veal, cook until browned all over. Transfer dish to hot oven, bake veal, uncovered, about 15 minutes or until veal is tender, cool.

Cut snake beans into 8cm lengths. Boil, steam or microwave snake beans until tender; drain, rinse under cold water, drain. Add noodles to pan of boiling water, boil, uncovered, until tender, drain.

Combine reserved marinade, blended cornflour and water, sugar and soy sauce in pan, stir over heat until sauce boils and thickens slightly, cool. Combine noodles, adzuki beans and snake beans, serve with sliced veal and sauce.

Marinade: Peel rind from orange using a vegetable peeler. Combine rind and remaining ingredients in bowl.

Serves 4.

BABY BEETROOT AND PEPPERONI SALAD

Beans best prepared a day ahead; store, covered, at room temperature.

¾ cup (170g) dried borlotti beans
150g pepperoni salami
12 drained artichoke hearts, halved
300g baby mushrooms, quartered
3 bunches (about 15) baby beetroot

DRESSING
⅔ cup (160ml) extra virgin olive oil
2 tablespoons balsamic vinegar
2 tablespoons lemon juice
2 tablespoons seeded mustard
½ teaspoon sugar

Place beans in bowl, cover well with water, cover, stand overnight.

Drain beans, add beans to pan of water, simmer, uncovered, about 35 minutes or until tender, drain well. Cut salami into 5mm slices, then cut each piece in half. Combine beans, salami, artichoke hearts, mushrooms and ⅓ cup (80ml) of the dressing in bowl, cover, refrigerate several hours or overnight.

Trim leaves from beetroot, reserve 16 leaves. Add reserved leaves to pan of boiling water, drain immediately, rinse under cold water, drain. Trim stalks about 3cm from beetroot. Boil, steam or microwave beetroot until tender; drain, peel.

Add bean mixture to pan, cook, stirring, until heated through, stir in reserved leaves. Serve bean mixture topped with beetroot; drizzle with remaining dressing.
Dressing: Combine all ingredients in screw-top jar; shake well.

Serves 4.

PIZZAS WITH SUN-DRIED TOMATOES AND PROSCIUTTO

2 teaspoons (7g) dried yeast
½ teaspoon sugar
¾ cup (180ml) warm water
2 cups (300g) plain flour
1 teaspoon salt
2 tablespoons olive oil
⅓ cup (about 100g) hummus

TOPPING
150g sliced prosciutto
¾ cup (80g) drained sun-dried tomatoes, sliced
⅔ cup (120g) black olives
2 tablespoons oil
4 green shallots, sliced
10 English spinach leaves, shredded
2 tablespoons shredded fresh basil

Combine yeast, sugar and water in small bowl, cover, stand in warm place about 10 minutes or until frothy.

Sift flour and salt into bowl, stir in yeast mixture and oil, mix to a soft dough. Turn dough onto lightly floured surface, knead about 5 minutes or until smooth.

Place dough in lightly oiled bowl, cover, stand in warm place about 1 hour or until dough is doubled in size.

Knead dough on floured surface until smooth. Divide dough into 4 portions. Roll each portion into a 16cm round, place rounds onto oiled oven trays, prick lightly with fork. Bake in hot oven about 10 minutes or until browned and crisp; cool. Spread 1 tablespoon of hummus onto each pizza base, spoon over topping.
Topping: Slice prosciutto into thin strips, add to dry pan, cook, stirring, until crisp; drain. Combine prosciutto and remaining ingredients in bowl; mix well.

Serves 4.

RIGHT: From left: Pizzas with Sun-Dried Tomatoes and Prosciutto, Baby Beetroot and Pepperoni Salad.

Plate and bowls from Mura Clay Gallery.

PEPPERED PORK WITH RASPBERRY VINAIGRETTE

600g pork fillets
1 tablespoon cracked
    black peppercorns
3 teaspoons dried juniper
    berries, crushed
2 tablespoons olive oil
½ bunch (about 320g) English
    spinach
1 small red oak leaf lettuce
1 small cos lettuce
200g fresh blueberries
200g fresh raspberries

RASPBERRY VINAIGRETTE
70g fresh raspberries
2 tablespoons raspberry vinegar
⅔ cup (160ml) olive oil
2 teaspoons sugar

Coat pork in combined peppercorns and juniper berries. Heat oil in pan, add pork, cook until browned all over. Transfer pork to wire rack in baking dish, bake, un-covered, in hot oven about 15 minutes or until pork is tender; cool. Serve sliced pork with torn spinach and lettuce leaves and berries; drizzle with raspberry vinaigrette.
Raspberry Vinaigrette: Blend or process berries until smooth, strain; discard seeds. Combine puree with remaining in-gredients in screw-top jar; shake well.

Serves 4 to 6.

BARBECUED PORK AND CHINESE CABBAGE SALAD

12cm piece (about 120g) fresh ginger
3 cloves garlic
oil for deep-frying
¼ bunch garlic chives
600g Chinese barbecued pork, sliced
1 medium Chinese cabbage, sliced
3 cups (about 240g) bean sprouts
1 cup (about 80g) snow pea sprouts
200g snow peas, halved diagonally
¾ cup (110g) roasted peanuts
½ cup whole fresh coriander leaves
½ cup whole fresh mint leaves

RED ONION PICKLE
½ cup (125ml) rice vinegar
¼ cup (60ml) mirin
¼ cup (60ml) dry red wine
1 clove garlic, sliced
pinch chilli flakes
2 tablespoons sugar
¼ teaspoon cracked
    black peppercorns
1 medium red Spanish onion, sliced

DRESSING
⅓ cup (80ml) light soy sauce
2 tablespoons sesame oil
1 tablespoon sugar
⅓ cup (80ml) cider vinegar
⅓ cup (80ml) oil

Cut ginger into thin strips. Cut garlic into thin slices. Deep-fry ginger and garlic in hot oil until lightly browned; drain well. Cut garlic chives into 2cm lengths.
    Combine half the ginger and garlic with garlic chives, pork, cabbage, bean sprouts, snow pea sprouts, snow peas, peanuts, herbs, and red onion pickle in bowl, add dressing; mix well. Sprinkle with remaining ginger and garlic.
Red Onion Pickle: Combine vinegar, mirin, wine, garlic, chilli flakes, sugar and peppercorns in pan, simmer, uncovered, 2 minutes. Add onion, cook, covered, until onion is soft; cool. Drain onions, reserve ¼ cup pickling liquid for dressing.
Dressing: Combine reserved pickling liquid and remaining ingredients in screw-top jar; shake well.

Serves 6.

PICNIC LOAF

Recipe best prepared a day ahead; store, covered, in refrigerator.

1 large eggplant, sliced
coarse cooking salt
2 medium red peppers
1 medium green pepper
1 medium yellow pepper
2 tablespoons olive oil
30g butter
2 cloves garlic, crushed
4 medium zucchini, sliced
2 batard loaves
¼ cup (60ml) sun-dried tomato paste
160g sliced spicy salami
12 black olives, pitted, sliced
¼ cup (25g) drained sun-dried
    tomatoes, chopped

Sprinkle eggplant slices with salt, stand 1 hour. Rinse under cold water, pat dry with absorbent paper. Grill eggplant slices in batches until lightly browned.
    Cut peppers in half lengthways, remove seeds and membranes. Grill peppers, skin side up, until skin blisters and black-ens. Peel away skin, cut peppers into strips. Heat oil, butter and garlic in pan, add zucchini, cook in batches until lightly browned, drain on absorbent paper; cool.
    Cut loaves in half horizontally. Grill cut sides of bread until lightly toasted, brush evenly with tomato paste. Cover 2 bread halves with salami, top with eggplant, peppers, zucchini, olives, sun-dried tomatoes and remaining bread halves; wrap firmly in foil. Place loaves on tray, place weight on top to flatten loaves; refrigerate overnight.

Serves 6 to 8.

FAR LEFT: From back: Barbecued Pork and Chinese Cabbage Salad; Peppered Pork with Raspberry Vinaigrette.
LEFT: Picnic Loaf.

Far left: Plate and bowl from The Design Store; salad servers from Bibelot; tiles from Pazotti.

CREAMY GNOCCHI AND HAM SALAD

500g gnocchi
30g butter
2 cloves garlic, crushed
500g baby mushrooms, sliced
4 bacon rashers, chopped
500g broccoli, chopped
120g snow peas, sliced
250g ham pieces, chopped

DRESSING
½ cup (125ml) cream
2 tablespoons sour cream
1 teaspoon Dijon mustard
1 tablespoon seeded mustard
2 teaspoons honey
⅓ cup chopped fresh parsley

Add gnocchi to large pan of boiling water, boil, uncovered, until just tender, drain.

Heat butter in pan, add garlic and mushrooms, cook, stirring, until mushrooms are soft and liquid is evaporated; remove from pan. Add bacon to same pan, cook, stirring, until browned and crisp; drain on absorbent paper. Boil, steam or microwave broccoli until just tender; drain, rinse under cold water, drain well.

Combine gnocchi, mushroom mixture, bacon, broccoli, snow peas and ham in bowl, add dressing; mix gently.
Dressing: Combine all ingredients in bowl; mix well.

Serves 4.

PORK WITH RED CABBAGE AND RAISIN SALAD

Raisins best prepared a day ahead; store, covered, at room temperature.

½ cup (85g) raisins
¼ cup (60ml) port
½ medium red apple
1 medium green apple
600g roast pork, chopped
½ medium red cabbage, finely
    shredded
1½ cups (150g) pecans or walnuts
4 green shallots, sliced
1 tablespoon caraway seeds

DRESSING
1 egg yolk
2 tablespoons cider vinegar
2 tablespoons sweet alcoholic cider
1 teaspoon French mustard
2 tablespoons apple juice
1 cup (250ml) olive oil

Combine raisins and port in bowl, cover, stand several hours or overnight.

Drain raisins, discard port. Core apples, cut into thin wedges. Combine raisins, apples and remaining ingredients in bowl, add dressing; mix well.
Dressing: Blend egg yolk, vinegar, cider, mustard and juice until smooth, gradually add oil in thin stream while motor is operating, blend until slightly thickened.

Serves 6.

HAM AND PICKLED PEAR SALAD

500g sliced leg ham
2 cups (about 100g) firmly packed
    watercress sprigs
8 radishes, quartered
1 tablespoon pecans
    or walnuts, chopped

PICKLED PEARS
2 medium pears
2 tablespoons finely chopped
    fresh ginger
1 cup (250ml) water
2 cups (500ml) cider vinegar
1½ cups (375g) sugar
1 cinnamon stick
3 star anise
1 teaspoon cloves

DRESSING
⅓ cup (80ml) oil
2 tablespoons chopped fresh chives

Cut ham into thin strips. Combine ham, watercress, radishes, nuts and half the dressing in bowl; mix gently. Top with sliced pickled pears; drizzle with remaining dressing.
Pickled Pears: Peel pears, halve and remove cores. Combine ginger, water, vinegar, sugar, cinnamon, star anise and cloves in pan. Stir over heat without boiling until sugar is dissolved, add pears, simmer, covered, about 5 minutes or until pears are tender; cool in poaching liquid. Drain pears, reserve ⅔ cup (160ml) liquid for dressing.
Dressing: Combine reserved poaching liquid, oil and chives in screw-top jar; shake well.

Serves 4.

RIGHT: Clockwise from left: Ham and Pickled Pear Salad, Pork with Red Cabbage and Raisin Salad, Creamy Gnocchi and Ham Salad.

Plate, bowls and accessories from Bibelot.

SMOKED CHICKEN AND HAM WITH FIGS

2 medium avocados
1 tablespoon lemon juice
1 medium bunch curly endive
1 cup (about 50g) firmly packed
    watercress sprigs
4 smoked chicken breasts, sliced
12 slices double-smoked ham
4 fresh figs, halved
1/2 cup (75g) roasted
    hazelnuts, halved

DRESSING
1/4 cup (60ml) olive oil
1 tablespoon lemon juice
pinch sugar

Chop avocados into 4cm pieces, brush with lemon juice.

Place avocado, endive, watercress, chicken, ham, figs and nuts on plate; drizzle with dressing.

Dressing: Combine all ingredients in screw-top jar: shake well.

Serves 4.

LEFT: From back: Warm Chicken and Nectarine Salad, Smoked Chicken and Ham with Figs.
BELOW: Tropical Chicken Salad.

Left: Plates, place mat and serviette from Ivory Coast Travel and Safari; tiles from Pazotti.
Below: Bowl from Amy's Tableware; tiles from Pazotti.

WARM CHICKEN AND NECTARINE SALAD

2 medium oranges
2 medium tomatoes
2 medium nectarines
30g butter
4 chicken breast fillets
2 tablespoons red wine vinegar
1 small mignonette lettuce
1 small butter lettuce

ORANGE YOGURT DRESSING
2 tablespoons plain yogurt
1/4 cup (60ml) orange juice
2 tablespoons sour cream
2 teaspoons chopped fresh mint
1 tablespoon chopped fresh chives

Using a vegetable peeler, peel rind thinly from oranges, avoiding white pith; cut rind into thin strips. Cut tomatoes and nectarines into thin wedges.

Heat butter in pan, add chicken, cook until browned and tender. Remove chicken from pan, slice lengthways. Add vinegar and rind to pan, simmer, uncovered, 30 seconds.

Top torn lettuce leaves with tomatoes, nectarines and chicken; drizzle with rind mixture. Serve warm chicken and nectarine salad with orange yogurt dressing.

Orange Yogurt Dressing: Combine all ingredients in bowl, mix well; cover, refrigerate 30 minutes.

Serves 4.

TROPICAL CHICKEN SALAD

1 large lime
4 chicken breast fillets
2 cups (500ml) chicken stock
500g kumara
200g snow peas

DRESSING
2 tablespoons oil
1 medium onion, finely chopped
1 clove garlic, crushed
1/3 cup (80ml) lime juice
400ml can coconut cream
1/4 cup (15g) shredded coconut
2 teaspoons sugar

Using a vegetable peeler, peel rind thinly from lime, avoiding white pith, cut rind into thin strips. Place chicken in pan in single layer, pour over enough stock to barely cover chicken, simmer, uncovered, about 10 minutes, turning once, or until tender; cool in stock.

Cut kumara into 2cm pieces. Boil, steam or microwave kumara and snow peas separately until tender; drain, rinse under cold water, drain. Cut snow peas diagonally. Cut chicken into 2cm pieces. Combine rind, kumara, snow peas and chicken in bowl, add dressing; mix gently.

Dressing: Heat oil in pan, add onion and garlic, cook, stirring, until onion is soft. Add remaining ingredients, simmer, uncovered, about 5 minutes or until mixture is thickened slightly; cool.

Serves 4 to 6.

ORIENTAL CHICKEN AND PRAWN SALAD

Chicken can be marinated a day ahead; store, covered, in refrigerator.

500g chicken thigh fillets, thinly sliced
¼ cup (60ml) light soy sauce
1 tablespoon oyster sauce
½ teaspoon five spice powder
1 tablespoon dry sherry
2 cloves garlic, crushed
1 teaspoon grated fresh ginger
cornflour
oil for deep-frying
500g packet fresh egg noodles
500g cooked prawns
100g snow peas
2 cups (about 160g) bean sprouts
**230g can bamboo shoots,
     rinsed, drained**
80g snow pea sprouts
1 small red pepper, thinly sliced
**⅔ cup (90g) slivered
     almonds, toasted**

DRESSING
2 tablespoons light soy sauce
½ teaspoon sesame oil
⅓ cup (80ml) oil
1 teaspoon fish sauce
1 teaspoon honey
1 clove garlic, crushed
1 tablespoon lemon juice

Combine chicken, sauces, spice powder, sherry, garlic and ginger in bowl; cover, refrigerate several hours or overnight.

Drain chicken, discard marinade. Toss chicken in cornflour, shake away excess cornflour. Deep-fry chicken in batches in hot oil until well browned and tender; drain on absorbent paper.

Add noodles to pan of boiling water, boil, uncovered, until tender; drain, rinse under cold water, drain well. Shell prawns, leaving tails intact. Add peas to boiling water, cook 30 seconds; drain, rinse under cold water, drain well.

Combine chicken, noodles, prawns, peas, bean sprouts, bamboo shoots, snow pea sprouts, pepper and nuts in bowl, add dressing; mix well.

Dressing: Combine all ingredients in screw-top jar; shake well.

Serves 4.

CHICKEN AND PEPPERS WITH HAZELNUT DRESSING

2 medium yellow peppers
2 medium red peppers
2 medium green peppers
2 cloves garlic, crushed
1 tablespoon seeded mustard
4 chicken breast fillets
1 tablespoon hazelnut oil
40g butter
3 bunches (about 225g) sorrel

HAZELNUT DRESSING
⅓ cup (50g) hazelnuts
¼ cup (60ml) hazelnut oil
¼ cup (60ml) oil
2 tablespoons white wine vinegar
¼ cup (40g) sultanas
1 clove garlic, peeled, quartered
1 tablespoon fresh thyme sprigs
¼ teaspoon sugar

Quarter peppers, remove seeds and membranes. Grill peppers, skin side up, until skin blisters and blackens. Peel away skin, cut peppers into strips.

Spread combined garlic and mustard over both sides of chicken. Heat oil and butter in pan, add chicken, cook on both sides until browned and tender, drain on absorbent paper; cool. Cut chicken into long thin slices. Top sorrel leaves with chicken and peppers, drizzle with hazelnut dressing.

Hazelnut Dressing: Spread hazelnuts onto oven tray, bake in moderately hot oven 5 minutes. Place hazelnuts on tea towel, rub firmly to remove skins. Return hazelnuts to tray, bake further 3 minutes or until lightly browned.

Combine oils, vinegar, sultanas, garlic, thyme and sugar in screw-top jar, stand several hours. Just before serving, discard garlic, add hazelnuts; shake well.

Serves 4.

QUAIL WITH PROSCIUTTO AND PESTO DRESSING

8 quail
8 slices prosciutto
2 bunches (about 240g) rocket
½ cup (40g) parmesan cheese flakes
⅓ cup (50g) pine nuts, toasted

PESTO DRESSING
1 cup firmly packed fresh basil leaves
2 cloves garlic, crushed
2 tablespoons pine nuts
¼ cup (20g) grated parmesan cheese
¾ cup (180ml) olive oil

Using sharp knife or scissors, cut down each side of backbone of quail; flatten quail, discard backbones. Grill or barbecue quail until browned and tender. Grill prosciutto until lightly browned. Place quail and prosciutto on rocket, sprinkle with cheese flakes and nuts; drizzle with pesto dressing.

Pesto Dressing: Blend or process basil, garlic, nuts and cheese with ¼ cup of the oil until smooth. Gradually add remaining oil in a stream while motor is operating; blend until smooth.

Serves 4.

LEFT: Oriental Chicken and Prawn Salad.
RIGHT: From back: Quail with Prosciutto and Pesto Dressing, Chicken and Peppers with Hazelnut Dressing.

Left: Plate from Horgan Imports; salad servers from Java Bazaar; tiles from Country Floors.
Right: Glassware by Peter Crisp from Australian Craftworks.

CHICKEN TONNATO

4 chicken breast fillets
2 cups (500ml) chicken
 stock, approximately
2 medium red peppers
2 medium green peppers
1 medium red oak leaf lettuce
2 medium butter lettuce
1 tablespoon drained capers

TUNA MAYONNAISE
1 egg yolk
¼ cup (60ml) olive oil
¼ cup (60ml) oil
1 clove garlic, crushed
2 teaspoons lemon juice
1 tablespoon drained
 capers, chopped
185g can tuna, drained

Place chicken in pan in single layer, add enough stock to barely cover chicken. Simmer, uncovered, about 10 minutes, turning once, or until chicken is tender; cool chicken in stock.

Cut peppers in half, remove seeds and membranes, grill peppers, skin side up, until skin blisters and blackens. Peel away skin, cut peppers into 2cm strips. Cut chicken lengthways into thin slices. Serve chicken on lettuce leaves with peppers and capers; top with tuna mayonnaise.
Tuna Mayonnaise: Blend or process egg yolk until smooth. Add combined oils gradually in a thin stream while motor is operating; add garlic, juice, capers and tuna, blend until smooth.

Serves 4.

MARINATED CHICKEN AND GOATS' CHEESE SALAD

5 chicken breast fillets, sliced
2 tablespoons light soy sauce
2 tablespoons olive oil
2 tablespoons lemon juice
1 tablespoon seasoned pepper
1 tablespoon olive oil, extra
500g green beans
1 cup (150g) unsalted
 roasted cashews
100g goats' cheese, crumbled

DRESSING
1 tablespoon Dijon mustard
2 tablespoons balsamic vinegar
⅓ cup (80ml) olive oil
2 green shallots, chopped
1 tablespoon lemon juice

Combine chicken, sauce, oil, juice and pepper in bowl, cover, refrigerate 1 hour.

Heat extra oil in pan, add undrained chicken in batches, cook until tender; cool. Cut beans into 4cm pieces. Boil, steam or microwave beans until just tender; drain, rinse under cold water, drain.

Combine chicken, beans and nuts in bowl, add dressing, mix well; serve sprinkled with cheese.
Dressing: Combine all ingredients in screw-top jar; shake well.

Serves 4.

CURRIED CHICKEN AND PASTA SALAD

2 cups (160g) shell pasta
1 tablespoon oil
2 tablespoons curry powder
4 green shallots, chopped
1 small red pepper, chopped
1 small green pepper, chopped
½ cup (125ml) mayonnaise
½ cup (125ml) light sour cream
2 cups (400g) chopped
 cooked chicken
8 butter lettuce leaves

Add pasta to large pan of boiling water, boil, uncovered, until tender; drain, rinse under cold water, drain.

Heat oil in pan, add curry powder, shallots and peppers, cook, stirring, 1 minute; cool. Combine pasta, curry mixture, mayonnaise, cream and chicken in bowl; mix well. Serve curried chicken mixture on lettuce leaves.

Serves 4.

LEFT: Clockwise from top: Curried Chicken and Pasta Salad, Marinated Chicken and Goats' Cheese Salad, Chicken Tonnato.

Plates and salad servers from Butler and Co., glass background from Cydonia Glass Studio.

WARM CHICKEN LIVER AND PISTACHIO SALAD

30g butter
500g chicken livers
1 tablespoon chopped fresh thyme
¼ cup (60ml) red wine vinegar
1 tablespoon olive oil
⅓ cup (50g) pistachios, toasted
20g butter, extra
1½ bunches (about 375g) mizuna
200g fresh raspberries

Heat butter in pan, add livers and thyme, cook, stirring, about 4 minutes or until livers are browned and tender; remove livers from pan. Add vinegar, oil and pistachios to pan, cook, stirring, until mixture boils, reduce heat, quickly stir in extra butter. Top mizuna with livers, drizzle with pistachio mixture, serve with raspberries.
Serves 4.

TURKEY, PEPPER AND TARRAGON SALAD

3 bacon rashers, chopped
2 large red peppers
3 sticks celery
400g sliced roast turkey
¾ cup (125g) brazil nuts, toasted, chopped
4 drained artichoke hearts, sliced
3 cups (about 150g) firmly packed watercress sprigs

TARRAGON DRESSING
2 tablespoons chopped fresh tarragon
2 teaspoons honey
2 tablespoons white vinegar
⅓ cup (80ml) olive oil

Add bacon to dry pan, cook, stirring, until bacon is crisp; drain on absorbent paper.
Quarter peppers, remove seeds and membranes. Grill peppers, skin side up, until skin blisters and blackens. Peel away skin, slice peppers thinly. Cut celery into 6cm thin strips. Cut turkey into thin strips.
Combine bacon, peppers, celery, turkey, nuts, artichokes and watercress in bowl; drizzle with tarragon dressing.
Tarragon Dressing: Combine all ingredients in screw-top jar; shake well.
Serves 4.

BELOW: From left: Turkey, Pepper and Tarragon Salad, Warm Chicken Liver and Pistachio Salad.
RIGHT: From left: Smoked Turkey and Witlof Salad, Chicken and Crispy Noodles with Peanut Sauce.

Below: Plates from Amy's Tableware.
Right: Soapstone salad bowl and hand-painted material from African Heritage.

CHICKEN AND CRISPY NOODLES WITH PEANUT SAUCE

35g rice vermicelli noodles
oil for deep-frying
425g can young corn spears, drained
2½ cups (about 500g) sliced
   cooked chicken
¾ cup (95g) cooked peas
1⅓ cups (100g) shredded
   red cabbage
1⅓ cups (100g) shredded
   savoy cabbage
1 cup (80g) bean sprouts
4 green shallots, chopped
150g oyster mushrooms, sliced
5 fresh dates, pitted, chopped

PEANUT SAUCE
⅓ cup (80ml) smooth peanut butter
⅓ cup (80ml) coconut cream
2 teaspoons light soy sauce
1½ teaspoons sugar
1½ teaspoons lime juice
⅓ cup (80ml) water, approximately

Break noodles in half, deep-fry in hot oil until puffed and crisp; drain.

Lightly crush noodles. Cut corn in half lengthways. Combine noodles and corn with remaining ingredients in bowl; drizzle with peanut sauce.

Peanut Sauce: Combine peanut butter, cream, sauce, sugar and lime juice in bowl, stir in enough water to give a thin pouring sauce.

Serves 4.

SMOKED TURKEY AND WITLOF SALAD

500g sliced smoked turkey breast
40g butter
2 tablespoons hazelnut oil
1 clove garlic, crushed
1 medium red apple
6 medium witlof
⅓ cup (35g) roasted
   hazelnuts, chopped
2 tablespoons chopped fresh chives

DRESSING
¼ cup (60ml) hazelnut oil
2 tablespoons oil
¼ cup (60ml) raspberry vinegar
½ teaspoon sugar
¼ teaspoon seasoned pepper

Cut turkey into thin strips. Heat butter and oil in pan, add turkey and garlic, cook, stirring, until turkey is lightly browned; drain well. Cut apple into thin strips.

Combine turkey, apple, witlof leaves and nuts in bowl; drizzle with dressing, sprinkle with chives.

Dressing: Combine all ingredients in screw-top jar; shake well.

Serves 4.

HERRING, POTATO AND EGG SALAD

4 (about 200g) rollmop herrings
10 baby new potatoes
2 medium apples, halved, sliced
12 drained cocktail onions
5 canned drained baby
    beets, quartered
6 hard-boiled eggs, halved

DRESSING
½ cup (125ml) mayonnaise
¼ cup (60ml) sour cream
2 tablespoons white wine vinegar
1 tablespoon chopped fresh dill

Unroll herrings, remove gherkins. Reserve gherkins for dressing. Cut herrings into strips. Boil, steam or microwave potatoes until tender; drain, cool.

Combine potatoes, apples and half the dressing in bowl; mix gently. Top potato mixture with herrings, onions, beets and eggs; drizzle with remaining dressing.

Dressing: Combine reserved chopped gherkins and remaining ingredients in bowl; mix well.

Serves 4 to 6.

RIGHT: from left: Herring, Potato and Egg Salad, Poached Fish and Mango with Tandoori Dressing.

Glassware by Margot Alexander available from Australian Craftworks.

POACHED FISH AND MANGO WITH TANDOORI DRESSING

Fish can be marinated a day ahead; store, covered, in refrigerator.

1 teaspoon fish sauce
1 teaspoon light soy sauce
1 tablespoon white vinegar
1 teaspoon sugar
4 (about 800g) firm white fish fillets
⅔ cup (160ml) water
½ large mango, sliced
6 radicchio lettuce leaves
1 small cos lettuce, shredded
160g snow pea sprouts
1 small yellow pepper, sliced

TANDOORI DRESSING
½ large mango, chopped
⅓ cup (80ml) plain yogurt
½ teaspoon sugar
½ teaspoon grated fresh ginger
1 teaspoon lemon juice
1 tablespoon oil
¼ teaspoon turmeric
¼ teaspoon paprika
¼ teaspoon garam masala
¼ teaspoon ground cardamom
pinch chilli powder
small pinch ground saffron

Combine sauces, vinegar and sugar in bowl, add fish, cover, refrigerate several hours or overnight.

Drain fish, reserve marinade. Combine reserved marinade and water in pan, bring to boil, add fish, simmer, covered, until fish is just tender. Drain fish on wire rack, discard poaching liquid. Break fish into pieces. Combine fish, mango, lettuce, sprouts and pepper on plate, top with tandoori dressing.

Tandoori Dressing: Blend or process mango flesh, yogurt, sugar, ginger and juice until smooth. Heat oil in pan, add spices, cook, stirring, until fragrant. Combine mango mixture and spice mixture in bowl, mix well; cover, refrigerate 1 hour.

Serves 4.

CHILLI CRAB AND GRAPEFRUIT SALAD

6 large (about 2.5kg) cooked
   blue swimmer crabs
1 cup (50g) firmly packed
   watercress sprigs
1 medium bunch curly endive
2 medium grapefruit, segmented
¾ cup (110g) roasted
   unsalted cashews
2 tablespoons shredded
   coconut, toasted

DRESSING
1 teaspoon fish sauce
1 teaspoon sambal oelek
1 tablespoon lime juice
½ cup (125ml) coconut milk
1 tablespoon chopped
   fresh coriander

Remove flesh from crab bodies and legs. Combine watercress, endive, grapefruit and nuts in bowl, top with crab flesh; drizzle with dressing, sprinkle with coconut.
Dressing: Combine all ingredients in screw-top jar; shake well.
Serves 4.

MARINATED BABY OCTOPUS WITH RED CABBAGE

Octopus can be marinated a day ahead; store, covered, in refrigerator.

1kg baby octopus
2 cloves garlic, crushed
⅓ cup (80ml) hoi sin sauce
2 tablespoons dry sherry
1 teaspoon grated fresh ginger
2 tablespoons oil
1 medium red pepper, sliced thinly
1 medium green pepper, sliced thinly
½ small red cabbage, shredded

DRESSING
¼ cup (60ml) rice wine vinegar
1½ tablespoons black bean sauce
⅓ cup (80ml) oil
½ teaspoon sambal oelek

Remove and discard heads and beaks from octopus. Cut octopus in half. Combine octopus, garlic, sauce, sherry and ginger in bowl; cover, refrigerate several hours or overnight.
   Heat oil in pan, add undrained octopus in batches, cook until browned and tender. Serve warm octopus with combined peppers and cabbage; drizzle with dressing.
Dressing: Combine all ingredients in screw-top jar; shake well.
Serves 4.

LEFT: From top: Chilli Crab and Grapefruit Salad, Marinated Baby Octopus with Red Cabbage.
RIGHT: Tuna and Braised Onion Salad.

Left: Plates and background from Cydonia Glass Studio; spoon from Dinosaur Designs.
Right: Bowl from Dinosaur Designs.

TUNA AND BRAISED ONION SALAD

¼ cup (60ml) oil
30g butter
3 large onions, sliced
2 tablespoons red wine vinegar
4 (about 600g) tuna steaks
1 bunch (about 120g) rocket
½ bunch (about 325g) English
   spinach, shredded

Heat oil and butter in heavy-based pan, add onions, cook, covered, stirring occasionally, about 30 minutes or until onions are very soft. Add vinegar, simmer, uncovered, 1 minute. Add tuna to same pan, cook, uncovered, until tuna is cooked as desired. Remove tuna from pan, cut into pieces. Serve warm tuna with braised onions, rocket and spinach.
Serves 4.

FRESH SNAPPER AND SNOW PEA SALAD

2 medium firm tomatoes, peeled, seeded
4 medium zucchini
1 small red pepper
¼ cup (40g) finely chopped pitted black olives
2 green shallots, chopped
60g butter
1 tablespoon olive oil
500g snapper fillets
100g snow peas, thinly sliced
1 medium butter lettuce

DRESSING
¼ cup (60ml) champagne vinegar
⅔ cup (160ml) virgin olive oil
2 teaspoons seeded mustard
1 teaspoon honey
1 clove garlic, crushed

Finely chop tomatoes, zucchini and pepper; combine in bowl. Stir in olives, shallots and ¼ cup (60ml) of the dressing.

Heat butter and oil in pan, add fish, cook until tender, cool. Slice fish into 2cm strips. Add snow peas, fish and torn lettuce leaves to tomato mixture, mix gently; drizzle with remaining dressing.
Dressing: Combine all ingredients in screw-top jar; shake well.
Serves 4.

FRESH SALMON AND PASTA SALAD

170g pasta shells
1 medium carrot, finely chopped
2 sticks celery, finely chopped
⅓ cup (80ml) mayonnaise
2 tablespoons sour cream
½ teaspoon grated lemon rind
¼ teaspoon fish sauce
1 tablespoon lemon juice
500g salmon fillets

DRESSING
¼ cup (60ml) lemon juice
¼ cup (60ml) olive oil
1 teaspoon chopped fresh dill

Add pasta to pan of boiling water, boil, uncovered, until just tender; drain. Combine pasta, carrot, celery, mayonnaise, sour cream, rind, sauce and juice in bowl; cover, refrigerate 1 hour.

Cook salmon in greased, heavy-based pan or on well-greased barbecue plate until tender. Remove skin from salmon; break salmon into pieces. Top pasta salad with salmon; drizzle with dressing.
Dressing: Combine all ingredients in screw-top jar; shake well.
Serves 4.

LEFT: From left: Fresh Salmon and Pasta Salad, Fresh Snapper and Snow Pea Salad.

Coloured bowls from Casa Shopping; salad servers from Dinosaur Designs; lattice bowl from Cydonia Glass Studio for The Glass Artist's Gallery.

OPEN HERB RAVIOLI WITH PRAWNS AND PESTO

We used dill, flat-leafed parsley, purple basil, unsprayed marigold, nasturtium and rose petals in this recipe.

⅔ cup (100g) plain flour
1 egg
1 teaspoon olive oil
¼ cup fresh herb leaves and
    flower petals
1.2kg cooked medium prawns
1 medium green oak leaf lettuce
1 bunch (about 250g) mizuna
½ cup loosely-packed fresh
    purple basil leaves
2 small avocados, sliced
1 medium papaw, sliced

PESTO MAYONNAISE
1 cup firmly packed fresh basil leaves
2 tablespoons pine nuts, toasted
2 cloves garlic, crushed
¼ cup (20g) grated parmesan cheese
¼ cup (60ml) olive oil
2 egg yolks
1 teaspoon French mustard
2 teaspoons white vinegar
1 cup (250ml) grapeseed oil

Process flour, egg and oil until combined. Knead dough on lightly floured surface until smooth; cover, refrigerate 30 minutes.

Roll dough through thickest setting on pasta machine until smooth and elastic. Cut into 4 equal portions. Roll each portion through pasta machine until as thin as possible. Sprinkle herbs and flowers over 2 pieces of pasta. Lightly brush the 2 remaining pasta pieces with water, place over herbs, press to seal. Roll pasta once through thinnest setting of machine, cut into 12 x 10cm x 11cm rectangles; lightly dust with flour.

Add pasta to large pan of boiling water, simmer, uncovered, about 2 minutes or until just tender; drain, rinse under cold water, drain well. Brush each side of pasta with oil, place each sheet between layers of baking paper until needed.

Shell and devein prawns, leaving tails intact. Place 1 sheet of pasta on plate, top with some of the lettuce, mizuna, basil, prawns, avocado and papaw; drizzle with pesto mayonnaise, top with another pasta sheet. Repeat with remaining ingredients on individual plates.

Pesto Mayonnaise: Process basil, nuts, garlic, cheese and olive oil until smooth; reserve pesto. Process yolks, mustard and vinegar until smooth, gradually add grapeseed oil in a thin stream while motor is operating. Combine reserved pesto and mayonnaise in bowl; mix well.

Serves 6.

LEFT: Open Herb Ravioli with Prawns and Pesto.
RIGHT: Lobster Salad with Red Pepper Mousses.
Right: Plate and cutlery from The Bay Tree.

LOBSTER SALAD WITH RED PEPPER MOUSSES

4 medium (about 800g) uncooked
    lobster tails
40g butter
2 cloves garlic, crushed
1 large radicchio lettuce
1 bunch (250g) rocket
⅓ cup (35g) drained sun-dried
    tomatoes, sliced
⅓ cup shredded fresh basil leaves

RED PEPPER MOUSSES
4 medium (about 800g) red peppers
¼ cup (60ml) red wine vinegar
2 teaspoons chicken stock powder
1 teaspoon sugar
3 teaspoons gelatine
1½ tablespoons water
1 cup (250ml) thickened cream

DRESSING
⅓ cup (80ml) olive oil
1 tablespoon white wine vinegar
¼ teaspoon French mustard

Remove lobster meat from tails in 1 piece. Heat butter and garlic in pan, add lobster, cook until lightly browned all over. Place lobster on oven tray, brush with pan juices; bake, uncovered, in moderately hot oven about 8 minutes or until lobster is just tender; cool. Slice lobster thickly. Turn mousses onto plates, surround with torn lettuce leaves, rocket, tomatoes, basil and lobster; drizzle with dressing.

Red Pepper Mousses: Lightly oil 4 moulds (½ cup/125ml capacity). Quarter peppers, remove seeds and membranes. Grill peppers, skin side up, until skin blisters and blackens. Peel skin, chop peppers. Combine peppers, vinegar and stock powder in pan, simmer, uncovered, until peppers are soft and liquid evaporated. Blend or process peppers and sugar until smooth, push through sieve.

Sprinkle gelatine over water in cup, place in pan of simmering water, stir until dissolved; cool slightly. Combine pepper mixture and gelatine in bowl, refrigerate until partly set. Beat cream until soft peaks form, fold into pepper mixture in 2 batches. Divide mixture between prepared moulds, cover, refrigerate several hours or until set.

Dressing: Combine all ingredients in screw-top jar; shake well.

Serves 4.

SMOKED TROUT AND ENDIVE SALAD

3 small smoked trout
1 medium bunch curly endive
1 medium radicchio lettuce
1 small green oak leaf lettuce
1 cup (about 50g) firmly packed
    watercress sprigs
250g cherry tomatoes

DRESSING
¼ cup (60ml) olive oil
2 tablespoons cider vinegar
1 tablespoon lemon juice
1 tablespoon chopped fresh dill

Remove skin and bones from trout; flake flesh. Combine torn endive and lettuce leaves, watercress and tomatoes in bowl, top with trout; drizzle with dressing.
Dressing: Combine all ingredients in screw-top jar; shake well.
Serves 4.

ORIENTAL PRAWN, MUSHROOM AND CUCUMBER SALAD

2 x 250g packets Japanese dried
    noodles
1 tablespoon sesame oil
1kg cooked medium prawns
50g Chinese dried mushrooms
½ cup (125ml) light soy sauce
1 cup (250ml) water
1 tablespoon grated fresh ginger
2 cloves garlic, crushed
2 tablespoons brown sugar
½ teaspoon five spice powder
6 green shallots, chopped
1 cup (about 80g) bean sprouts
1 long thin green cucumber,
    thinly sliced

Add noodles to large pan of boiling water, boil, uncovered, until tender; drain, rinse under cold water, drain. Combine noodles and oil in bowl.

Shell and devein prawns, leaving tails intact. Place mushrooms in heatproof bowl, cover with boiling water, stand 20 minutes; drain mushrooms, discard liquid, trim away stems. Combine mushrooms, sauce, water, ginger, garlic, sugar and spice powder in pan, simmer, uncovered, about 5 minutes or until reduced by one-third. Combine noodle mixture, mushroom mixture, prawns, shallots and bean sprouts in bowl; mix well. Serve warm noodle mixture with cucumber.
Serves 4.

BELOW: From left: Oriental Prawn, Mushroom and Cucumber Salad, Smoked Trout and Endive Salad.
RIGHT: Nutty Sardines with Snow Pea Salad.

Below: Bowls from Parkers of Turramurra.
Right: Plate and wooden mat from Country Floors.

NUTTY SARDINES WITH SNOW PEA SALAD

16 (about 500g) fresh sardines
plain flour
2 eggs, lightly beaten
1½ cups (110g) stale breadcrumbs
½ cup (75g) finely
    chopped macadamias
2 teaspoons grated lemon rind
1 tablespoon chopped fresh thyme
oil for deep-frying

SNOW PEA SALAD
1 small leek
150g snow peas
⅔ cup (100g) macadamias,
    toasted, halved
½ cup (125ml) sour cream
1 teaspoon grated lemon rind
1½ tablespoons lemon juice
2 teaspoons chopped fresh thyme
½ teaspoon honey

LEMON DRESSING
1½ tablespoons lemon juice
2 tablespoons oil
1 teaspoon honey

Remove heads and entrails.
    Cut through underside to backbone; rinse under cold water. Cut backbone

through at tail end without piercing skin. Pull backbone out towards head end to remove. Remove small bones. Pat dry with absorbent paper.
    Toss sardines in flour, shake away excess flour. Dip sardines into egg then combined breadcrumbs, nuts, rind and thyme. Deep-fry sardines in hot oil until lightly browned; drain on absorbent paper. Serve sardines with snow pea salad and lemon dressing.

Snow Pea Salad: Cut leek and snow peas into thin strips. Combine leek, snow peas and remaining ingredients in bowl; mix well.

Lemon Dressing: Combine all ingredients in screw-top jar; shake well.

Serves 4.

SEAFOOD, POTATO AND WATER CHESTNUT SALAD

500g baby new potatoes, halved
100g sugar snap peas
60g green beans, halved
2 medium limes
800g uncooked medium prawns
⅓ cup (80ml) olive oil
6 cloves garlic, crushed
2 teaspoons cumin seeds
400g scallops
½ cup (125ml) lime juice
1 tablespoon honey
1 tablespoon chopped fresh mint
1 tablespoon chopped fresh coriander
227g can whole water chestnuts, sliced
1 medium green oak leaf lettuce

Boil, steam or microwave potatoes, peas and beans separately until just tender; drain, rinse under cold water, drain, cool.

Using vegetable peeler, peel rind thinly from limes, avoiding any white pith; cut rind into thin strips. Shell and devein prawns, leaving tails intact.

Heat oil in pan, add garlic and seeds, cook, stirring, until fragrant. Add prawns and scallops, cook, stirring, 2 minutes. Add rind, juice, honey and herbs, cook, stirring, until prawns and scallops are just cooked; cool. Combine potatoes, peas, beans, prawn mixture and water chestnuts in bowl, serve on lettuce leaves.

Serves 4.

SOY AND LEMON SEAFOOD WITH SESAME VEGETABLES

300g squid hoods
500g uncooked medium prawns
500g scallops
2 tablespoons light soy sauce
2 tablespoons lemon juice
1 tablespoon chopped lemon grass
2 tablespoons olive oil
1 tablespoon olive oil, extra

SESAME VEGETABLES
2 medium carrots
1 large red pepper
2 medium zucchini
2 sticks celery
6 spears fresh asparagus
20g butter
2 tablespoons sesame seeds, toasted

DRESSING
⅓ cup (80ml) olive oil
1 tablespoon lemon juice
1 tablespoon light soy sauce
¼ teaspoon sesame oil
pinch five spice powder
½ teaspoon sugar

Cut squid into 3cm pieces, mark inside surface of pieces in diamond pattern. Shell and devein prawns. Combine squid, prawns, scallops, sauce, juice, lemon grass and oil in bowl; mix well. Cover, refrigerate 1 hour. Drain, discard marinade.

Heat extra oil in pan, add seafood, cook, stirring, few minutes or until seafood is tender. Serve warm seafood with sesame vegetables; top with dressing.

Sesame Vegetables: Cut carrots, pepper, zucchini, celery and asparagus into thin strips. Heat butter in pan, add vegetables and seeds, stir-fry until vegetables are just tender.

Dressing: Combine all ingredients in screw-top jar; shake well.

Serves 4.

WARM SEAFOOD SALAD WITH CURRY BUTTER

We used unsprayed edible flower petals in this recipe; for example, borage, nasturtiums, lavender and rose petals.

600g cooked Balmain bugs
300g medium uncooked prawns
1 tablespoon oil
200g scallops
100g lambs' lettuce
1 small coral lettuce
1 small cos lettuce
½ cup fresh flower petals

CURRY BUTTER
200g butter
1 tablespoon curry powder
3 teaspoons honey
½ teaspoon French mustard
1 tablespoon chopped fresh coriander

DRESSING
1½ tablespoons red wine vinegar
½ teaspoon French mustard
⅓ cup (80ml) olive oil

Remove flesh from Balmain bug shells, discard shells, cut flesh in half lengthways. Shell and devein prawns, leaving tails intact.

Heat oil in pan, add prawns and scallops in batches, cook until just tender. Add Balmain bug flesh to pan, cook gently until heated through. Transfer seafood to shallow heatproof dish, top with curry butter, grill until butter just starts to melt. Combine torn lettuce leaves and dressing on plate, sprinkle with flower petals, top with seafood in curry butter.

Curry Butter: Beat butter in small bowl with electric mixer until light and fluffy, add curry powder, honey, mustard and coriander, beat until combined.

Dressing: Combine all ingredients in screw-top jar; shake well.

Serves 4.

FAR LEFT: From top: Seafood, Potato and Water Chestnut Salad, Soy and Lemon Seafood with Sesame Vegetables.
LEFT: Warm Seafood Salad with Curry Butter.

Far left: Plates by Mareen Cahill for The Glass Artist's Gallery; background glass from Cydonia Glass Studio.
Left: Plate from Opus Design.

CHILLI LIME SEAFOOD WITH SEED CRACKERS

Seafood best prepared a day ahead; store, covered, in refrigerator.

4 medium (about 400g) whiting fillets
500g uncooked medium prawns
2 eggs
2 tablespoons plain flour
1 teaspoon celery salt
oil for shallow-frying

MARINADE
½ cup (125ml) oil
2 teaspoons cumin seeds, crushed
2 teaspoons coriander seeds
2 cloves garlic, sliced
2 small fresh red chillies, finely chopped
1 teaspoon grated lime rind
⅓ cup (80ml) lime juice
⅓ cup (80ml) orange juice
½ cup (125ml) red wine vinegar
2 teaspoons sugar
1 teaspoon paprika

SAUTEED LEEKS
2 medium leeks
30g butter

SEED CRACKERS
1 cup (150g) plain flour
30g butter
1 egg, lightly beaten
1 tablespoon water
2 teaspoons milk
1 tablespoon coarse sea salt
1 tablespoon poppy seeds
1 tablespoon sesame seeds

Remove and discard skin and bones from fillets. Cut each fillet diagonally into 1cm strips. Shell and devein prawns, leaving tails intact. Combine eggs, flour and salt in bowl, beat until smooth. Add fish and prawns, mix lightly to coat.

Shallow-fry fish and prawns in batches in hot oil until lightly browned; drain on absorbent paper. Combine fish, prawns and marinade in shallow dish, cover, refrigerate several hours or overnight.

Drain fish and prawns, reserve marinade. Top sauteed leeks with fish and prawns; drizzle with reserved marinade. Serve with seed crackers.

Marinade: Heat oil in pan, add seeds, garlic and chillies, cook, stirring, until fragrant. Add remaining ingredients, simmer, uncovered, 2 minutes; cool 10 minutes.

Sauteed Leeks: Cut leeks into 6cm thin strips. Heat butter in pan, add leeks, cook, stirring, until just soft.

Seed Crackers: Sift flour into bowl, rub in butter, add egg and enough water to make ingredients cling together. Turn dough onto lightly floured surface, knead lightly until smooth. Divide dough into 4 portions, roll each portion out to 1mm thick. Place on lightly greased oven trays, brush with milk, sprinkle with combined salt, poppy and sesame seeds. Bake in moderate oven about 10 minutes or until well browned. Cool on wire rack.

Serves 4.

WARM SALAD OF MUSSELS AND LEEK

2kg small mussels
3 cloves garlic, crushed
½ cup (125ml) dry white wine
½ cup chopped fresh parsley
1 small leek
2 teaspoons balsamic vinegar
1 cup firmly packed flat-leafed parsley leaves, extra

TOMATO AND CUCUMBER SALSA
2 medium green cucumbers, peeled, seeded, chopped
4 large tomatoes, peeled, seeded, chopped
1 tablespoon sweet chilli sauce
2 cloves garlic, crushed
2 teaspoons grated fresh ginger
2 teaspoons balsamic vinegar

Scrub mussels, remove beards. Heat garlic, wine and parsley in large pan, add mussels, cook, covered, over high heat about 5 minutes or until mussels open; remove mussels from pan. Discard any unopened mussels. Return pan to heat, simmer, uncovered, until liquid is reduced to about ⅓ cup (80ml). Cut leek into rings, add leek and vinegar to pan, cook, stirring, until leek is just tender.

Remove and discard half of each mussel shell. Spoon warm leek mixture over mussels in shell, serve with extra parsley leaves and tomato and cucumber salsa.

Tomato and Cucumber Salsa: Combine all ingredients in bowl; mix well.

Serves 6.

LEFT: Chilli Lime Seafood with Seed Crackers.
BELOW: Warm Salad of Mussels and Leek.

Below: Plate from Opus Design.

51

ULTIMATE SALAD SANDWICH

½ cup firmly packed fresh basil
  leaves
1 tablespoon pine nuts
2 tablespoons grated
  parmesan cheese
2 tablespoons sour cream
8 slices wholegrain rye bread
2 hard-boiled eggs, sliced
1 medium cucumber, peeled,
  thinly sliced
1 medium carrot, finely grated
1 medium avocado, sliced
50g snow pea sprouts
1 cup (about 60g) lentil sprouts
½ cup (125ml) cottage cheese

Process basil and nuts until combined, add parmesan cheese and cream, process until smooth. Spread basil mixture evenly over 4 slices of bread, top with egg slices, cucumber, carrot, avocado, snow pea sprouts, lentil sprouts and cottage cheese. Add remaining bread slices.

Makes 4.

MINTED BARLEY AND FRESH TOMATO SALAD

1 cup (200g) barley
2 small green cucumbers,
  seeded, chopped
4 medium tomatoes, peeled,
  seeded, chopped
6 medium radishes, sliced
½ cup chopped fresh parsley
¼ cup chopped fresh mint
2 green shallots, chopped
1 small bunch curly endive

DRESSING
⅔ cup (160ml) olive oil
¼ cup (60ml) red wine vinegar
2 teaspoons brown sugar

Add barley to pan of boiling water, simmer, uncovered, until tender; drain, rinse under cold water, drain well. Combine barley, cucumbers, tomatoes, radishes, herbs, shallots and dressing in bowl. Serve salad with endive leaves.

Dressing: Combine all ingredients in screw-top jar; shake well.

Serves 2 to 4.

BLACK-EYED BEAN SALAD WITH BAGEL CROUTONS

Beans best prepared a day ahead; store, covered, at room temperature.

2 cups (400g) dried black-eyed beans
200g yellow squash, quartered
200g green squash, quartered
350g sugar snap peas

DRESSING
⅓ cup (80ml) red wine vinegar
1 tablespoon Dijon mustard
2 teaspoons sugar
⅔ cup (160ml) olive oil
2 cloves garlic, crushed

BAGEL CROUTONS
4 bagels, thinly sliced
125g butter, melted
1 tablespoon chopped fresh parsley
1 tablespoon chopped fresh thyme
1 teaspoon chopped fresh oregano
½ teaspoon garlic powder

Place beans in bowl, cover well with water, cover, stand overnight.

Drain beans, add to pan of boiling water, simmer, uncovered, until just tender; drain. Boil, steam or microwave squash and peas separately until just tender. Drain, rinse under cold water, drain well. Combine beans, squash, peas and dressing in bowl; mix well. Serve with bagel croutons.

Dressing: Combine all ingredients in screw-top jar; shake well.

Bagel Croutons: Brush both sides of sliced bagels with combined butter, herbs and garlic powder. Place on oven trays in single layer, bake in moderate oven about 10 minutes or until crisp.

Serves 4 to 6.

NUTTY TOFU AND POTATO SALAD

3 medium new potatoes
250g French beans, halved
375g packet firm tofu, drained
oil for deep-frying
2 small bunches (about 700g) bok
  choy, chopped
1 cup (about 80g) bean sprouts
1 small green cucumber, chopped

PEANUT DRESSING
1 tablespoon oil
1 small onion, finely chopped
1½ teaspoons curry powder
½ teaspoon ground cumin
1½ teaspoons sweet chilli sauce
2 teaspoons plain flour
½ cup (125ml) crunchy peanut butter
⅔ cup (160ml) vegetable stock
400ml can coconut milk
3 teaspoons brown sugar
¼ cup (35g) chopped unsalted
  roasted peanuts

Boil, steam or microwave potatoes and beans separately until tender; drain, rinse under cold water, drain well. Cut potatoes into quarters. Cut tofu into 2cm squares, pat dry on absorbent paper. Deep-fry tofu in batches in hot oil until lightly browned; drain on absorbent paper.

Combine potatoes, beans, tofu, bok choy, bean sprouts and cucumber in bowl; drizzle with hot peanut dressing.

Peanut Dressing: Heat oil in pan, add onion, cook, stirring, until soft. Add curry powder, cumin, sauce and flour, cook, stirring, 2 minutes. Stir in remaining ingredients, stir over heat until mixture boils and thickens slightly.

Serves 4.

LEFT: Ultimate Salad Sandwich.
RIGHT: Clockwise from left: Minted Barley and Fresh Tomato Salad, Black-Eyed Bean Salad with Bagel Croutons, Nutty Tofu and Potato Salad.

Left: Plate by Barbara Dimitri for Hamilton Design Glass Gallery; glass background from Hamilton Design Glass Gallery.
Right: Glass plates by Ozone.

RATATOUILLE SALAD

2 large red peppers
3 baby eggplants
½ cup (125ml) olive oil
3 medium egg tomatoes
1 large zucchini
2 tablespoons pine nuts, toasted
1½ tablespoons shredded fresh basil
⅓ cup (55g) small black olives

TOMATO VINAIGRETTE
1 large tomato
2 teaspoons olive oil
1 teaspoon white vinegar
ground black pepper

Quarter peppers, remove seeds and membranes. Grill peppers, skin side up, until skin blisters and blackens. Peel away skin, cut peppers into thin strips. Thinly slice eggplants lengthways.

Heat oil in pan, add eggplant in batches, cook until lightly browned; drain on absorbent paper. Slice tomatoes lengthways; discard seeds. Cut zucchini into 5cm matchsticks. Pour tomato vinaigrette onto 4 plates, top with peppers, eggplants, tomatoes and zucchini, sprinkle with nuts, basil and olives.
Tomato Vinaigrette: Blend or process all ingredients until well combined, push through sieve; discard seeds.

Serves 2 to 4.

HERBED CHICK PEA SALAD WITH PITTA CRISPS

2 pitta pocket breads
310g can chick peas, rinsed, drained
2 small green cucumbers,
    seeded, chopped
2 medium tomatoes, peeled,
    seeded, chopped
3 green shallots, sliced
⅓ cup (55g) black olives,
    pitted, quartered
½ cup chopped fresh mint
½ cup chopped fresh coriander
1 medium cos lettuce, shredded
½ cup (125ml) plain yogurt

DRESSING
½ cup (125ml) olive oil
¼ cup (60ml) lemon juice
1 clove garlic, crushed
1 teaspoon sugar

Split bread in half, place in single layer on oven tray, bake in moderate oven 10 minutes, turn bread, continue cooking further 10 minutes or until lightly browned and dry. Break bread into pieces.

Combine chick peas, cucumbers, tomatoes, shallots, olives, herbs and lettuce in bowl, add dressing; mix well. Serve salad with yogurt and pitta crisps.
Dressing: Combine all ingredients in screw-top jar; shake well.

Serves 4.

SAFFRON RICE AND NUTTY TOFU SALAD

45g ghee
1 tablespoon grated fresh ginger
2 cloves garlic, crushed
1 teaspoon sambal oelek
1 teaspoon coriander seeds, crushed
1 teaspoon cumin seeds, crushed
½ teaspoon cardamom seeds
2 cinnamon sticks
1½ cups (300g) basmati rice
3 cups (750ml) boiling water
tiny pinch ground saffron
1 large vegetable stock cube
45g ghee, extra
½ cup (80g) unsalted macadamias
½ cup (80g) almond kernels
½ cup (25g) flaked coconut, toasted
1 tablespoon sugar

FRIED TOFU
297g packet firm tofu
plain flour
oil for deep-frying

Heat ghee in pan, add ginger, garlic, sambal oelek, seeds and cinnamon sticks, cook, stirring, until fragrant. Add rice, water, saffron and crumbled stock cube, simmer, uncovered, until almost all liquid is evaporated. Cover, cook over low heat about 10 minutes, remove from heat, stand, covered, further 10 minutes. Discard cinnamon sticks.

Heat extra ghee in pan, add nuts, cook, stirring, until browned. Combine rice, nut mixture, coconut, sugar and fried tofu in bowl; mix gently. Serve warm or cold.
Fried Tofu: Drain tofu on absorbent paper, cut into 1½cm cubes. Toss cubes in flour, shake away excess flour. Deep-fry tofu in hot oil until browned; drain well.

Serves 4.

RIGHT: Clockwise from left: Herbed Chick Pea Salad with Pitta Crisps, Saffron Rice and Nutty Tofu Salad, Ratatouille Salad.

China from Primex Products Pty. Ltd.

FELAFEL ROLLS WITH HUMMUS AND SALAD

¾ cup (150g) dried broad beans
¾ cup (150g) dried chick peas
1 small onion, chopped
2 cloves garlic, chopped
2 teaspoons ground coriander
1 teaspoon ground cumin
¼ teaspoon paprika
pinch cayenne pepper
2 tablespoons chopped fresh parsley
oil for deep-frying
6 rounds Lebanese bread
1 medium iceberg lettuce, shredded
2 medium tomatoes, sliced
2 small green cucumbers, sliced
1 medium red Spanish onion, sliced

HUMMUS
439g can chick peas, rinsed, drained
2 cloves garlic, crushed
⅓ cup (80ml) lemon juice
⅓ cup (80ml) tahini
1 tablespoon water

YOGURT DRESSING
1 cup (250ml) plain yogurt
1 clove garlic, crushed
2 tablespoons chopped fresh parsley

Place beans in bowl, cover well with cold water, cover, stand 48 hours, change water once. Place chick peas in bowl, cover well with cold water, cover, stand 15 hours.

Drain beans, peel and discard skins. Drain chick peas. Process beans, chick peas, onion and garlic until finely minced. Transfer mixture to bowl, stir in coriander, cumin, paprika, cayenne pepper and parsley. Roll 2 level tablespoons of mixture into balls, stand 30 minutes. Deep-fry felafel in hot oil until browned and cooked; drain on absorbent paper.

Heat Lebanese bread in moderate oven 5 minutes, spread with hummus, top with lettuce, tomatoes, cucumbers , onion and warm felafel. Drizzle with yogurt dressing, roll up firmly.

Hummus: Process all ingredients until smooth and creamy.

Yogurt Dressing: Combine all ingredients in bowl; mix well.

Serves 6.

BROCCOLI AND CAULIFLOWER WITH TAHINI DRESSING

800g broccoli, chopped
800g cauliflower, chopped
1 large red pepper, finely chopped
2½ cups (about 150g) lentil sprouts

TAHINI DRESSING
⅓ cup (80ml) tahini
2 tablespoons lemon juice
½ cup (125ml) water
⅓ cup (80ml) olive oil
1 teaspoon sugar
½ teaspoon garlic salt

Boil, steam or microwave broccoli and cauliflower until just tender; drain, rinse under cold water, drain well. Combine broccoli, cauliflower, pepper and sprouts in bowl; drizzle with tahini dressing.

Tahini Dressing: Blend or process tahini, juice and water until pale and thick; stir in remaining ingredients.

Serves 4.

FETA RAVIOLI WITH ARTICHOKES AND EGGPLANT

2 cups (300g) plain flour
3 eggs
2 teaspoons olive oil

FILLING
150g feta cheese
60g packaged cream cheese
1½ tablespoons sour cream
2 teaspoons chopped fresh thyme
2 teaspoons chopped fresh chives

DRESSING
2 tablespoons balsamic vinegar
½ cup (125ml) olive oil
1 clove garlic, crushed

ARTICHOKE AND EGGPLANT SALAD
2 medium red peppers
1 large eggplant, sliced
oil for deep-frying
375g jar artichokes, drained
2 medium tomatoes, peeled,
   seeded, sliced
2 tablespoons chopped fresh oregano
½ cup firmly packed flat-leafed
   parsley leaves

Process flour, eggs and oil until combined. Turn onto lightly floured surface, knead until smooth. Cover, refrigerate 30 minutes. Divide dough into 4 pieces, roll 2 pieces separately until 2mm thick.

Place teaspoons of filling 4cm apart over 1 sheet of pasta. Lightly brush second pasta sheet with water, place over filling, press firmly between filling. Cut into square ravioli shapes; lightly sprinkle with flour. Repeat with remaining dough and filling.

Add ravioli to large pan of boiling water, simmer, uncovered, about 2 minutes or until just tender; drain, rinse under cold water; drain. Toss ravioli in half the dressing, reserve remaining dressing for artichoke and eggplant salad. Serve ravioli with artichoke and eggplant salad.

Filling: Process cheeses, cream and herbs until just combined.

Dressing: Combine all ingredients in screw-top jar; shake well.

Artichoke and Eggplant Salad: Quarter peppers, remove seeds and membranes. Grill, skin side up, until skin blisters and blackens. Peel skin, slice peppers. Deep-fry eggplant in hot oil until browned; drain. Combine peppers, eggplant, reserved dressing and remaining ingredients in bowl; mix well.

Serves 4 to 6.

LEFT: From left: Felafel Rolls with Hummus and Salad, Broccoli and Cauliflower with Tahini Dressing.
RIGHT: From back: Potato Baskets with Chilli Pepper Dressing, Feta Ravioli with Artichokes and Eggplant.

Left: Glass by Erna Messenger for Hamilton Design Glass Gallery.
Right: Glass plates by Allan Crynes for Hamilton Design Glass Gallery.

POTATO BASKETS WITH CHILLI PEPPER DRESSING

3 large (about 600g) potatoes, grated
1 tablespoon plain flour
1 egg yolk
1 teaspoon seasoned pepper
⅓ cup (80ml) oil

VEGETABLE SALAD
200g snow peas
2 medium carrots
4 cups (about 320g) bean sprouts
1 tablespoon light soy sauce
½ teaspoon sesame oil

CHILLI PEPPER DRESSING
1 large red pepper
½ cup (125ml) olive oil
¼ cup (60ml) sweet chilli sauce

Combine potatoes, flour, yolk and pepper in bowl; mix well. Heat 1 tablespoon of the oil in pan, add quarter of the potato mixture, flatten to a 16cm round, cook until browned underneath, turn, cook until browned on other side. Repeat with remaining oil and potato mixture.

Press warm potato rounds over up-turned individual pie dishes on oven tray. Bake in moderately hot oven about 20 minutes or until potato baskets are firm; turn onto wire rack to cool. Serve potato baskets with vegetable salad and chilli pepper dressing.

Vegetable Salad: Cut peas and carrots into thin strips of the same length. Combine vegetables, bean sprouts, sauce and oil in bowl; mix well.

Chilli Pepper Dressing: Quarter peppers, remove seeds and membranes. Grill peppers, skin side up, until skin blisters and blackens. Peel away skin, chop peppers. Blend or process peppers, oil and sauce until smooth.

Serves 4.

TWICE-BAKED VEGETABLES AND RICE SALAD

2 tablespoons olive oil
1 medium red pepper, quartered
1 medium green pepper, quartered
6 baby eggplants, halved
4 cloves garlic, halved
1 medium lemon
1 medium red Spanish onion, sliced
½ cup (125ml) olive oil, extra
¼ cup (60ml) lemon juice
1 cup (200g) brown rice
⅓ cup fresh mint leaves
⅓ cup fresh flat-leafed parsley leaves
1 small green cucumber, sliced

TAHINI SAUCE
⅔ cup (160ml) orange juice
1 tablespoon lemon juice
⅓ cup (80ml) tahini

Combine oil, peppers, eggplants and garlic in baking dish, stir until vegetables are coated with oil. Bake, covered, in moderately hot oven 15 minutes, uncover, bake further 15 minutes or until vegetables are tender.

Using a vegetable peeler, peel rind thinly from lemon, avoiding any white pith; cut rind into fine strips. Combine vegetables, rind strips, onion, extra oil and juice in bowl, cover, refrigerate several hours.

Add rice to pan of boiling water, boil, uncovered, about 30 minutes or until just tender, drain.

Place vegetable mixture in baking dish, bake, covered, in moderately hot oven about 12 minutes or until heated through. Stir in herbs and cucumber. Serve vegetables warm or cold with rice and tahini sauce.

Tahini Sauce: Beat juices and tahini in small bowl until pale and thickened slightly.

Serves 4.

PICKLED BABY BEETROOT WITH HASH BROWNS

Beetroot best pickled a week ahead; store in sealed jar in a cool, dark cupboard.

12 (about 1kg) baby beetroot
¾ cup (160g) sugar
¾ cup (180ml) red wine vinegar
½ cup (125ml) white vinegar
¼ cup (60ml) dry red wine
2 teaspoons black peppercorns
1 teaspoon yellow mustard seeds
4 sprigs lemon thyme

HASH BROWNS
30g butter
1 medium onion, finely chopped
1 clove garlic, crushed
5 medium potatoes, grated
2 tablespoons Dijon mustard
3 teaspoons chopped fresh
    lemon thyme
1 teaspoon grated lemon rind
plain flour
¼ cup (60ml) oil

MUSTARD CRESS DRESSING
⅓ cup (80ml) olive oil
2 tablespoons lemon juice
2 teaspoons yellow mustard seeds
½ teaspoon sugar
1 tablespoon mustard cress

Trim leaves about 3cm from beetroot. Add unpeeled beetroot to large pan of boiling water, simmer, uncovered, about 40 minutes or until tender. Peel beetroot; pack into sterilised jar.

Combine sugar, vinegars, wine, peppercorns, yellow mustard seeds and thyme in pan, stir over heat, without boiling, until sugar is dissolved. Pour pickling liquid over beetroot to cover completely; seal while hot.

Remove beetroot from liquid, discard liquid. Cut beetroot into quarters, serve warm or cold with hash browns; drizzle with mustard cress dressing.

Hash Browns: Heat butter in pan, add onion and garlic, cook, stirring, until onion is soft. Add potatoes, stir until potatoes are sticky, remove from heat, stir in mustard, thyme and rind. Shape mixture into 4 x 10cm patties with wet hands. Toss patties in flour, shake away excess flour. Heat oil in pan, add hash browns, cook about 10 minutes each side or until lightly browned and cooked through.

Mustard Cress Dressing: Combine all ingredients in screw-top jar; shake well.

Serves 4.

LEFT: From left: Twice-Baked Vegetables and Rice Salad, Pickled Baby Beetroot with Hash Browns.

Plates from Primex Products Pty. Ltd.

CORIANDER TOFU SALAD WITH SPICY DRESSING

2 x 375g packets firm tofu
oil for deep-frying
12 sprigs fresh coriander
1 bunch (about 250g) fresh
** asparagus spears, chopped**
2 medium carrots
½ small red Spanish onion, sliced
8 small radishes, sliced
1 cup (about 80g) bean sprouts
227g can water chestnuts,
** drained, halved**
⅓ cup (50g) unsalted
** roasted peanuts**

SPICY DRESSING
½ cup (125ml) oil
⅓ cup (80ml) lime juice
2 tablespoons chopped
** fresh coriander**
1 tablespoon chopped fresh
** lemon grass**
1 small fresh red chilli, finely chopped
1 tablespoon light soy sauce
3 teaspoons sugar
1 clove garlic, crushed

Wrap tofu in 3 sheets of absorbent paper, weigh down with plate; stand 4 hours. Cut tofu into 2cm x 5cm lengths. Deep-fry tofu in batches in hot oil until browned; drain on absorbent paper. Deep-fry coriander in batches until bright green; drain on absorbent paper. Boil, steam or microwave asparagus until just tender; drain, rinse under cold water, drain. Cut carrot into long, thin strips. Combine all ingredients and spicy dressing in bowl; mix well.

Spicy Dressing: Combine all ingredients in screw-top jar; shake well.

Serves 4 to 6.

CORN PANCAKES WITH SALSA AND GUACAMOLE

440g can corn kernels
⅔ cup (100g) plain flour
3 eggs

SALSA
2 medium limes
4 medium tomatoes, peeled, seeded,
** thinly sliced**
1 small red Spanish onion,
** thinly sliced**
1 medium red pepper, thinly sliced
1 medium green pepper, thinly sliced
½ small fresh red chilli,
** finely chopped**
2 tablespoons chopped
** fresh coriander**
1 clove garlic, crushed
2 tablespoons lime juice
½ teaspoon sugar
2 tablespoons olive oil
1 tablespoon tomato puree

GUACAMOLE
1 large ripe avocado,
** roughly chopped**
1 clove garlic, crushed
1 tablespoon lime juice
½ small fresh red chilli, seeded,
** finely chopped**
2 tablespoons sour cream

Drain corn, reserve ⅓ cup (70g) corn. Process flour, eggs and remaining corn until smooth; stir in reserved corn. Pour heaped tablespoons of batter into heated greased heavy-based pan, cook until lightly browned underneath, turn, cook other side. Serve warm with salsa and guacamole.

Salsa: Using a vegetable peeler, peel rind thinly from limes, avoiding white pith; cut rind into thin strips. Combine rind, tomatoes, onion, peppers, chilli and coriander in bowl. Add combined garlic, juice, sugar, oil and puree; mix well.

Guacamole: Process avocado, garlic, juice and chilli until smooth, add sour cream, process until just combined.

Serves 4.

BELOW: From left: Coriander Tofu Salad with Spicy Dressing, Corn Pancakes with Salsa and Guacamole.
RIGHT: From left: Nutty Carrot, Currant and Burghul Salad, Herb Gnocchi with Cauliflower and Almonds.

Below and right: China from Primex Products Pty. Ltd.

NUTTY CARROT, CURRANT AND BURGHUL SALAD

⅓ cup (55g) burghul
4 medium carrots, grated
½ cup (75g) currants
½ cup (70g) slivered
   almonds, toasted
⅓ cup chopped fresh coriander

DRESSING
2 tablespoons olive oil
2 tablespoons lime juice
1 teaspoon ground cumin
½ teaspoon ground cinnamon
½ teaspoon sugar

Place burghul in bowl, cover with boiling water, stand 15 minutes; drain. Pat burghul dry between layers of absorbent paper. Combine burghul with remaining ingredients in bowl, add dressing; mix well.
Dressing: Combine all ingredients in screw-top jar; shake well.

Serves 2 to 4.

HERB GNOCCHI WITH CAULIFLOWER AND ALMONDS

300g cauliflower, chopped
⅓ cup (55g) blanched
   almonds, toasted

HERB GNOCCHI
4 large (about 750g) old potatoes
1 egg, lightly beaten
¼ cup (40g) fine semolina
¼ cup chopped fresh basil
¼ cup chopped fresh chives
⅓ cup (25g) grated parmesan cheese
1¼ cups (185g) plain flour

TOMATO DRESSING
⅓ cup (80ml) white vinegar
¾ cup (180ml) oil
½ teaspoon sugar
2 teaspoons Dijon mustard
2 green shallots, finely chopped
2 medium tomatoes, peeled,
   seeded, chopped

Boil, steam or microwave cauliflower until tender; drain, cool. Combine cauliflower, herb gnocchi and tomato dressing in bowl; mix gently, sprinkle with nuts.
Herb Gnocchi: Boil, steam or microwave potatoes until tender; drain. Push potatoes through sieve into large bowl. Stir in egg, semolina, herbs, cheese and enough flour to mix to a soft dough. Knead dough on floured surface until smooth. Shape level teaspoons of dough into balls. Place ball in palm of hand, press floured fork onto balls of dough to make indentations and flatten slightly. Repeat with remaining dough.

Add gnocchi to large pan of boiling water, simmer, uncovered, about 3 minutes or until tender; drain, rinse under cold water, drain well.
Tomato Dressing: Combine all ingredients in bowl; mix well.

Serves 4.

BRAISED ARTICHOKE AND CAULIFLOWER SALAD

8 small fresh artichokes
⅔ cup (160ml) olive oil
10 green shallots, chopped
150g baby mushrooms, chopped
1 small green cucumber, chopped
4 sticks celery, chopped
1 bay leaf
10 black peppercorns
10 coriander seeds
2 tablespoons tomato paste
2 cloves garlic, crushed
2 tablespoons lemon juice
1⅓ cups (330ml) dry white wine
½ cup (125ml) water
2 medium tomatoes, chopped
1 tablespoon fresh chervil sprigs

CAULIFLOWER SALAD
⅓ cup (80ml) olive oil
1 small cauliflower, chopped
2 cloves garlic, crushed
½ cup (125ml) dry white wine
½ cup (125ml) water
1 tablespoon lemon juice
2 sprigs fresh thyme
1 bay leaf
pinch ground saffron
10 coriander seeds

Trim base of artichokes so they sit flat. Remove tough outer leaves and trim remaining leaves.

Pull away inside leaves and coarse centre with spoon.

Heat oil in pan, add artichokes, shallots, mushrooms, cucumber and celery, cook, stirring, 5 minutes. Tie bay leaf, peppercorns and seeds in a small piece of muslin. Add muslin bag, paste, garlic, juice,

wine and water to pan. Simmer, covered, about 45 minutes or until artichokes are tender. Discard muslin bag.

Spoon some of the vegetable mixture into artichokes, serve with remaining vegetable mixture and cauliflower salad; sprinkle with tomato and chervil. Serve warm or cold.

Cauliflower Salad: Heat oil in pan, add cauliflower, cook, covered, stirring occasionally, 4 minutes. Add remaining ingredients, simmer, uncovered, about 10 minutes or until liquid is evaporated. Discard thyme and bay leaf.

Serves 4.

SWEET CHILLI NUT BALL SALAD

310g can butter beans,
    rinsed, drained
1 cup (145g) unsalted roasted
    cashews
¼ cup (60ml) smooth peanut butter
1½ teaspoons sambal oelek
1 egg
2 tablespoons light soy sauce
1 teaspoon paprika
1 cup (70g) stale breadcrumbs
oil for deep-frying
1 bunch (about 250g) fresh
    asparagus spears
½ x 375g packet thin egg noodles
250g cherry tomatoes

SWEET CHILLI SAUCE
⅓ cup (75g) sugar
1 tablespoon white vinegar
¼ cup (60ml) water
2 teaspoons chopped fresh
    lemon grass
1 small fresh red chilli, sliced
3 teaspoons lime juice
1 tablespoon fresh coriander leaves

Blend or process beans, nuts, peanut butter, sambal oelek, egg, sauce, paprika and breadcrumbs until smooth. Roll 2 level teaspoons of mixture into balls. Deep-fry nut balls in batches in hot oil until lightly browned and crisp; drain on absorbent paper.

Cut asparagus into 4cm lengths. Boil, steam or microwave asparagus until tender; drain, rinse under cold water, drain well. Add noodles to pan of boiling water, boil until tender, drain. Combine asparagus, noodles and tomatoes in bowl, top with nut balls; drizzle with sweet chilli sauce.

Sweet Chilli Sauce: Combine sugar, vinegar, water and lemon grass in pan, cook, stirring, until sugar is dissolved; simmer, uncovered, about 3 minutes or until sauce thickens slightly. Stir in chilli, juice and coriander.

Serves 4

RIGHT: From left: Braised Artichoke and Cauliflower Salad, Sweet Chilli Nut Ball Salad.

Plates from Accoutrement.

GOLDEN PUMPKIN SHELLS WITH CURRIED KUMARA

6 medium golden nugget pumpkins
¼ cup (60ml) oil
1.5kg kumara
250g broccoli, chopped
6 green shallots, chopped
4 hard-boiled eggs, sliced
⅔ cup (100g) unsalted
    roasted cashews
½ cup (125ml) sour cream

CURRY MAYONNAISE
8 egg yolks
¾ cup (180ml) lemon juice
3 teaspoons curry powder
2 teaspoons ground cumin
2 teaspoons ground coriander
2 teaspoons garam masala
2 teaspoons ground cardamom
2 cups (500ml) oil

Cut tops from pumpkins, scoop out seeds; discard seeds. Stand pumpkins in ovenproof dish, add enough boiling water to come 1cm up sides of pumpkins, replace tops of pumpkins; brush with oil. Bake, covered, in moderately hot oven about 45 minutes or until tender, remove pumpkins from dish; cool.

Cut kumara into 2cm pieces, place on oven tray. Bake, uncovered, in hot oven about 30 minutes or until just tender; cool. Boil, steam or microwave broccoli until just tender; drain, rinse under cold water, drain well.

Combine kumara, broccoli, shallots, eggs, nuts and sour cream in bowl; stir in curry mayonnaise. Serve curried kumara mixture in pumpkin shells.
Curry Mayonnaise: Blend or process egg yolks, juice and spices until smooth. Gradually add oil in a thin stream while motor is operating, blend until thick.

Serves 6.

PEPPERED FETTUCCINE WITH TOMATOES AND BOCCONCINI

250g fettuccine pasta
250g spinach fettuccine pasta
1 small red Spanish onion, sliced
250g bocconcini, chopped
2 tablespoons drained green
    peppercorns, rinsed
250g cherry tomatoes, halved
⅓ cup chopped fresh basil
⅔ cup (160ml) olive oil
⅓ cup (80ml) white wine vinegar
1 clove garlic, crushed
1 tablespoon shredded fresh basil

Add pasta to large pan of boiling water, boil, uncovered, until just tender; drain, rinse under cold water, drain well. Combine pasta, onion, bocconcini, peppercorns, tomatoes and chopped basil in large bowl. Add combined oil, vinegar and garlic; mix well. Sprinkle with shredded basil.

Serves 4.

MEXICAN SALAD ROLL-UPS

4 pieces lavash bread
½ small iceberg lettuce, shredded
4 hard-boiled eggs, sliced
2 medium tomatoes, chopped
1 small green pepper, chopped
1 small onion, sliced
1 cup (125g) grated tasty cheese
¼ cup (60ml) sour cream

BEAN SPREAD
1 tablespoon oil
2 medium onions, finely chopped
1 tablespoon sambal oelek
750g can red kidney beans, rinsed,
    drained, mashed

AVOCADO SPREAD
2 medium avocados, peeled, mashed
2 cloves garlic, crushed
1 tablespoon lemon juice
dash tabasco sauce

Spread each piece of bread evenly with bean spread and avocado spread, top with lettuce, eggs, tomatoes, pepper, onion, cheese and sour cream. Roll up firmly to enclose filling.
Bean Spread: Heat oil in pan, add onions, cook, stirring, until soft. Add sambal oelek, cook, stirring, 1 minute. Add beans, stir until well combined; cool.
Avocado Spread: Combine all ingredients in bowl; mix well.

Serves 4.

RIGHT: Clockwise from left: Golden Pumpkin Shells with Curried Kumara, Mexican Salad Roll-Ups, Peppered Fettuccine with Tomatoes and Bocconcini.

Plates from Century Universe.

DEEP-FRIED CREPE PARCELS WITH SALAD LEAVES

1 egg, lightly beaten
1 egg yolk
1½ teaspoons oil
½ cup (75g) plain flour
¾ cup (180ml) milk
plain flour, extra
oil for deep-frying, extra
1 bunch (about 120g) rocket
2 cups (about 100g) firmly packed
　watercress sprigs

FILLING
1 small zucchini
1 medium carrot
10g butter
2 cloves garlic, crushed
60g baby mushrooms, quartered
1 cup (about 100g) mung beans
60g snow peas, thinly sliced
½ cup (60g) grated tasty cheese
½ cup (75g) roasted unsalted
　cashews, chopped

BATTER
3 eggs, lightly beaten
¼ cup (35g) plain flour

DRESSING
1½ tablespoons lemon juice
2 tablespoons oil
1 tablespoon roasted unsalted
　cashews, chopped

Combine egg, egg yolk, oil and flour in bowl. Gradually add milk, beating well after each addition; beat until smooth, cover, stand 30 minutes.

Pour 2 tablespoons of batter into heated greased heavy-based pan, cook until browned underneath. Turn crepe, brown other side. Repeat with remaining batter. You will need 6 crepes.

Divide filling into 6 portions. Place 1 portion of filling onto centre of crepe, fold in ends, roll up to enclose filling. Repeat with remaining crepes and filling. Carefully coat filled crepes in extra flour, shake away excess flour. Dip crepes into batter, deep-fry in hot extra oil until browned and crisp, drain on absorbent paper. Serve crepes sliced with rocket and watercress; drizzle with dressing.

Filling: Cut zucchini and carrot into matchsticks. Heat butter in pan, add garlic and mushrooms, cook, stirring, until mushrooms are soft; cool. Combine mushroom mixture, zucchini, carrot and remaining ingredients in bowl; mix well.

Batter: Combine all ingredients in bowl, beat until smooth.

Dressing: Combine ingredients in screw-top jar; shake well.

Serves 6.

PICKLED VEGETABLES WITH DEEP-FRIED BOCCONCINI

Pickled vegetables can be made a week ahead; store, covered, in refrigerator.

500g bocconcini
plain flour
2 eggs, lightly beaten
2 cups (140g) stale breadcrumbs
2 teaspoons seasoned pepper
oil for deep-frying
1 medium cos lettuce
1 medium green oak leaf lettuce
⅓ cup (80ml) olive oil

PICKLED VEGETABLES
1 medium carrot
1 small green cucumber
1 small onion
½ medium red pepper
½ medium yellow pepper
100g cauliflower, chopped
60g broccoli, chopped
¼ teaspoon yellow mustard seeds
1 teaspoon dill seeds
½ teaspoon fennel seeds
1 teaspoon black peppercorns
¾ cup (180ml) white wine vinegar
⅓ cup (80ml) dry white wine
⅓ cup (80ml) water
⅓ cup (80ml) honey
1 tablespoon sugar

Slice bocconcini into 1cm pieces. Toss bocconcini in flour, shake away excess flour, dip into eggs then combined breadcrumbs and pepper. Deep-fry bocconcini in hot oil until lightly browned; drain on absorbent paper. Serve bocconcini with torn lettuce and pickled vegetables. Combine reserved pickling liquid (from pickled vegetables) and oil in screw-top jar; shake well, drizzle dressing over salad.

Pickled Vegetables: Cut carrot and cucumber into thin strips, slice onion. Cut peppers into 2cm squares. Boil, steam or microwave carrot, cauliflower and broccoli until just tender, rinse under cold water; drain well.

Combine seeds, peppercorns, vinegar, wine, water, honey and sugar in pan, simmer, uncovered, 5 minutes. Combine vegetables in bowl, pour over hot pickling liquid, mix well; cool, cover, refrigerate at least 2 days. Strain vegetables, reserve ⅓ cup (80ml) pickling liquid for dressing.

Serves 6.

LEFT: Deep-Fried Crepe Parcels with Salad Leaves.
RIGHT: Pickled Vegetables with Deep-Fried Bocconcini.

Left: Plates from The Craft Centre.
Right: Plates from Century Universe.

JAPANESE EGG AND SUSHI RICE BASKETS

8 sheets nori seaweed
400g raw tuna fillet, thinly sliced
1 small green cucumber, thinly sliced
1 medium avocado, sliced
2 tablespoons pink pickled ginger
50g salmon roe
wasabi paste

SUSHI RICE
4 cups (800g) white short-grain rice
1.125 litres (4½ cups) water
1 strip konbu seaweed
½ cup (125ml) rice vinegar
2½ tablespoons sugar
2½ teaspoons salt

OMELETTE
20g butter
2 eggs, beaten

SAUCE
¼ cup (60ml) light soy sauce
2 tablespoons mirin
1 teaspoon brown sugar
3 teaspoons sesame seeds, toasted

Layer 2 sheets of nori seaweed together at an angle.

Press layered nori between 2 lightly oiled medium heatproof bowls, place bowls on oven tray, bake in moderate oven 5 minutes; cool.

Gently remove nori from between bowls, taking care to retain shape. Repeat layering and baking with remaining nori. Spoon sushi rice into nori baskets, top with omelette strips, tuna, cucumber, avocado, ginger, roe and wasabi to taste; drizzle with sauce.

Sushi Rice: Rinse rice under cold water until water becomes clear. Cover rice with water, stand 1 hour; drain well.

Combine rice, water and seaweed in pan, bring to boil, simmer, covered, over low heat 18 minutes. Remove pan from heat, stand, covered, further 10 minutes; remove and discard seaweed. Turn rice into glass bowl, cool slightly. Combine vinegar, sugar and salt in pan, stir over heat until sugar is dissolved. Stir vinegar mixture into rice; cool.

Omelette: Heat quarter of the butter in small heavy-based pan. Pour quarter of the eggs into pan, cook omelette until lightly browned underneath. Turn omelette, brown other side. Repeat 3 times more with remaining butter and eggs. Cool omelettes, cut into 1cm strips.

Sauce: Combine all ingredients in screw-top jar; shake well.

Serves 4.

GOUDA CHEESE AND RED SALAD PIZZA

27cm frozen pizza base
250g gouda cheese, chopped
1 tablespoon olive oil

RED SALAD
1 small radicchio lettuce, shredded
1 small red Spanish onion, sliced
1 small red pepper, sliced
1 medium tomato, sliced
1 teaspoon sambal oelek
2 tablespoons balsamic vinegar
2 tablespoons olive oil

Place pizza base on oven tray, bake in moderately hot oven about 20 minutes or until browned and crisp. Top pizza base with combined red salad and cheese, bake in moderately hot oven about 10 minutes or until cheese is melted and topping warm; drizzle with oil.
Red Salad: Combine all ingredients in bowl; mix well. Stand salad 15 minutes, drain, discard dressing.

Serves 2.

POACHED EGGS ON SPINACH WITH ANCHOVY MAYONNAISE

½ small French bread stick
¾ cup (60g) grated parmesan cheese
1 teaspoon oil
4 bacon rashers, finely chopped
1½ bunches (about 980g) English spinach
4 eggs, poached

ANCHOVY MAYONNAISE
3 egg yolks
2 tablespoons lemon juice
3 anchovy fillets
1 teaspoon French mustard
½ cup (125ml) grapeseed oil
½ cup (125ml) olive oil
2 tablespoons water

Cut bread into thin slices, place on oven tray, sprinkle with cheese, bake in moderately hot oven about 10 minutes or until browned and crisp. Heat oil in pan, add bacon, cook until crisp; drain on absorbent paper.

Combine spinach, half the anchovy mayonnaise and half the bacon in bowl. Divide mixture between 4 plates, top with warm poached egg, drizzle with remaining anchovy mayonnaise, sprinkle with remaining bacon. Serve with croutons.
Anchovy Mayonnaise: Process yolks, juice, anchovies and mustard until smooth, slowly add combined oils in a thin stream while motor is operating; add water, process until smooth.

Serves 4.

SPICY RISONI SALAD WITH OMELETTE ROLLS

2 cups (430g) risoni pasta
6 eggs
750g pumpkin
⅓ cup (80ml) oil
2 medium onions, sliced
1 clove garlic, crushed
½ teaspoon ground cinnamon
1 teaspoon ground ginger
½ teaspoon ground coriander
1 teaspoon garam masala
pinch ground saffron
½ cup (100g) red lentils
1½ cups (375ml) water
250g mushrooms, sliced
1 medium green pepper, chopped
8 fresh dates, sliced

Add pasta to large pan of boiling water, boil, uncovered, until tender, drain.

Lightly beat 2 of the eggs, add to small greased heavy-based pan, cook until set; remove from pan. Repeat twice more with remaining eggs. Roll up omelettes tightly, slice thinly.

Cut pumpkin into 2cm pieces. Heat oil in pan, add onions, garlic and spices, cook, stirring, until onions are soft. Add pumpkin, lentils, water, mushrooms and pepper, cook, uncovered, stirring occasionally, until vegetables are tender. Add pasta and dates, stir until well combined. Serve with omelette rolls. Serve warm or cold.

Serves 4.

FAR LEFT: From back: Gouda Cheese and Red Salad Pizza, Japanese Egg and Sushi Rice Baskets.
LEFT: From back: Spicy Risoni Salad with Omelette Rolls, Poached Eggs on Spinach with Anchovy Mayonnaise.

Far left: Glass plates from H. A. G. Imports; tiles from Country Floors.
Left: Glass by Velta Vilmanis for Hamilton Design Glass Gallery; tile from Hamilton Design Glass Gallery.

LAYERED ITALIAN SALAD

3 medium red peppers
1 medium eggplant
4 medium zucchini
⅓ cup (80ml) olive oil
30g butter
500g baby mushrooms, sliced
1 cup firmly packed fresh
    basil leaves
200g mozzarella cheese, sliced
1 cup (160g) black olives,
    pitted, halved
2 medium tomatoes, sliced

GARLIC DRESSING
½ cup (125ml) olive oil
¼ cup (60ml) white vinegar
1 teaspoon sugar
2 cloves garlic, crushed

Quarter peppers, remove seeds and membranes. Grill peppers, skin side up, until skin blisters and blackens; peel skin. Cut eggplant and zucchini lengthways into ½cm slices. Place eggplant and zucchini on oven tray, brush with oil, grill until well browned.

Heat butter in pan, add mushrooms, cook, stirring, until moisture is evaporated.

Place eggplant over base of dish (6 cup/1.5 litre capacity). Top with layer of peppers, basil, zucchini, cheese, olives, mushrooms and tomatoes; drizzle with garlic dressing. Cover, refrigerate several hours or overnight.
Garlic Dressing: Combine all ingredients in screw-top jar; shake well.

Serves 4.

CRISP FRIED POTATO SALAD

1.5kg baby potatoes
1 tablespoon oil
1 tablespoon oil, extra
2 medium onions, sliced
250g sugar snap peas
250g feta cheese
1 small red oak leaf lettuce

VINAIGRETTE
½ cup (125ml) olive oil
¼ cup (60ml) white wine vinegar
2 teaspoons seeded mustard
1 clove garlic, crushed
1 tablespoon chopped fresh chives

Boil, steam or microwave potatoes until tender, drain, cut potatoes in half. Heat oil on barbecue or in pan, add potatoes, cook on cut side until browned and crisp; drain on absorbent paper. Heat extra oil in pan, add onions, cook, stirring, until soft; drain on absorbent paper.

Boil, steam or microwave peas until just tender; drain, rinse under cold water, drain well. Cut cheese into small cubes. Combine potatoes, onions, peas and cheese in bowl, add vinaigrette; mix gently. Top lettuce leaves with potato mixture.
Vinaigrette: Combine all ingredients in screw-top jar; shake well.

Serves 4 to 6.

SMOKED TURKEY AND STILTON CHEESE SALAD

1 tablespoon oil
1 medium red Spanish onion, sliced
½ teaspoon sugar
150g sugar snap peas
1 small mignonette lettuce, shredded
1 small radicchio lettuce, shredded
150g smoked turkey, chopped
150g Stilton cheese, crumbled
180g pumpernickel bread, chopped

DRESSING
75g Stilton cheese, finely chopped
⅔ cup (160ml) thickened cream
½ cup (125ml) light sour cream
1 tablespoon cracked
    black peppercorns

Heat oil in heavy-based pan, add onion, cook, covered, stirring occasionally, until soft. Add sugar, stir until onions are lightly browned; drain on absorbent paper. Boil, steam or microwave peas until just tender; drain, rinse under cold water, drain well. Combine onion mixture, peas, torn lettuce leaves, turkey, cheese and bread in bowl; drizzle with dressing.
Dressing: Combine all ingredients in bowl; mix well.

Serves 4 to 6.

LEFT: Layered Italian Salad.
ABOVE: From back: Smoked Turkey and Stilton Cheese Salad, Crisp Fried Potato Salad.

Above: Glass trays from Shirley Gibson for Hamilton Design Glass Gallery.

GRILLED GOATS' CHEESE ON RYE CROUTES

360g goats' cheese
6 slices dark rye bread
2 teaspoons olive oil
2 medium witlof
1 large bunch curly endive
1 medium apple, sliced
⅓ cup (50g) hazelnuts,
  toasted, halved
2 tablespoons chopped fresh chives

THYME BUTTER
50g butter
1 clove garlic, crushed
2 teaspoons chopped fresh thyme
pinch cracked black peppercorns

HAZELNUT DRESSING
2 tablespoons red wine vinegar
¼ cup (60ml) olive oil
¼ cup (60ml) hazelnut oil

Cut cheese into 6 slices using a hot knife. Spread bread with thyme butter, place on oven tray, bake in moderately hot oven about 10 minutes or until underside of bread just starts to brown. Top croutes with cheese, brush with oil, grill until lightly browned and heated through.

Serve goats' cheese croutes with witlof leaves, torn endive leaves and apple, drizzle with hazelnut dressing, sprinkle with nuts and chives.
Thyme Butter: Blend or process all ingredients until well combined.
Hazelnut Dressing: Combine all ingredients in screw-top jar; shake well.

Serves 4 to 6.

CAESAR SALAD SANDWICH

1 teaspoon oil
3 bacon rashers, chopped
8 slices wholemeal bread, toasted
¾ cup (75g) walnuts,
  toasted, chopped
1 small cos lettuce
4 hard-boiled eggs, sliced
¼ cup (20g) parmesan cheese flakes

ANCHOVY BUTTER
2 x 56g cans anchovy fillets, drained
2 teaspoons Dijon mustard
2 tablespoons olive oil
40g soft butter
2 cloves garlic, crushed

DRESSING
½ teaspoon grated lemon rind
1½ tablespoons lemon juice
1 clove garlic, crushed
⅓ cup (80ml) olive oil

Heat oil in pan, add bacon, cook until crisp; drain on absorbent paper. Spread each slice of toast with anchovy butter, sprinkle with nuts, press on firmly. Top 4 slices of toast with torn lettuce, egg slices, bacon and cheese; drizzle with dressing, cover with remaining toast.
Anchovy Butter: Blend or process all ingredients until well combined.
Dressing: Combine all ingredients in screw-top jar; shake well.

Serves 4.

WARM OKRA, EGG AND ROMANO CHEESE SALAD

8 eggs
30g butter
250g okra
150g sugar snap peas
100g piece romano cheese
1 medium red oak leaf lettuce
1 medium radicchio lettuce
3 cups (150g) firmly packed
  watercress sprigs
125g butter, extra, melted
2 tablespoons balsamic vinegar

Place eggs in pan, cover with cold water. Bring to boil, stirring, then simmer, uncovered, 5 minutes. Drain, cover with cold water, stand 5 minutes. Peel eggs, cut into quarters lengthways.

Heat butter in pan, add okra, cook, stirring, about 3 minutes or until just tender. Add peas, cook, stirring, until warm.

Using a vegetable peeler, cut flakes from cheese. Combine lettuce, watercress and cheese, top with warm okra mixture and eggs, drizzle with combined extra butter and vinegar.

Serves 4.

FAR LEFT: From back: Caesar Salad Sandwich, Grilled Goats' Cheese on Rye Croutes.
LEFT: Warm Okra, Egg and Romano Cheese Salad.

Far left: Plates from Century Universe.
Left: Plate from The Craft Centre.

ACCOMPANIMENTS

You'll find a terrific range of delicious accompaniments here. All the recipes are intended as side dishes which will transform the simplest meal into something much more special – whether it be a fresh salad made from a variety of leaves to dress up a humble grilled chop, or an interesting curried fruit salad to accompany roast beef. Just mix and match to suit your tastes and the occasion. We have included rice, pasta and pulses, vegetables, plus green, leafy salads and a selection of unusual and appetising fruit salads. Most of the dressings can be made a day ahead, but the salads are best made just before serving.

TOASTED BARLEY TABBOULEH

¾ cup (150g) barley
1½ cups firmly packed flat-leafed
    parsley, chopped
¼ cup chopped fresh mint
½ small green cucumber, chopped
1 medium tomato, chopped
4 green shallots, chopped
⅓ cup (80ml) oil
2 tablespoons lemon juice
1 clove garlic, crushed

Place barley in dry pan, stir over heat until lightly browned; remove from heat. Add barley to pan of boiling water, simmer, uncovered, about 25 minutes or until tender; drain well, cool. Combine barley with remaining ingredients in bowl; mix well.
Serves 6.

LEFT: Clockwise from left: Potato, Corn and Bean Salad, Butter Bean, Egg and Salami Salad, Toasted Barley Tabbouleh.

BUTTER BEAN, EGG AND SALAMI SALAD

50g sliced salami
2 x 310g cans butter beans,
    rinsed, drained
1 medium tomato, peeled,
    seeded, chopped
1 small onion, finely chopped
⅓ cup shredded fresh basil
1 hard-boiled egg, finely grated
1 anchovy fillet, chopped

DRESSING
⅓ cup (80ml) olive oil
2 tablespoons balsamic vinegar
½ teaspoon sugar

Cut salami into thin strips. Combine salami, beans, tomato, onion, basil and dressing in bowl; mix well. Top with egg and anchovy.
Dressing: Combine all ingredients in screw-top jar; shake well.
Serves 4 to 6.

POTATO, CORN AND BEAN SALAD

1kg baby new potatoes, halved
440g can corn kernels,
    rinsed, drained
310g can butter beans,
    rinsed, drained
4 green shallots, chopped
1 tablespoon chopped fresh chives

DRESSING
⅓ cup (80ml) olive oil
2 tablespoons lemon juice
½ cup (125ml) mayonnaise
½ cup (125ml) sour cream
1 teaspoon sugar
1 tablespoon Dijon mustard

Boil, steam or microwave potatoes until tender; drain, cool. Combine potatoes with remaining ingredients in bowl, add dressing; mix well.
Dressing: Combine all ingredients in bowl; whisk until smooth.
Serves 4 to 6.

PASTA WITH BEANS AND TANGY ONION RELISH

150g penne pasta
150g green beans

ONION RELISH
2 tablespoons oil
1 large red Spanish onion, sliced
⅓ cup (80ml) white vinegar
⅓ cup (80ml) dry red wine
⅓ cup (65g) brown sugar

Add pasta to large pan of boiling water, boil, uncovered, until just tender; drain. Slice beans, boil, steam or microwave beans until just tender; drain, rinse under cold water, drain well. Combine pasta, beans and onion relish in bowl; mix lightly.
Onion Relish: Heat oil in pan, add onion, cook, stirring, until onion is soft. Add remaining ingredients, simmer, uncovered, 10 minutes, cool.
Serves 6.

MINTED COUSCOUS WITH PEAS AND MUSTARD SEEDS

2 teaspoons oil
2 teaspoons black mustard seeds
40g butter
2¼ cups (560ml) vegetable stock
1½ cups (270g) couscous
1 cup (125g) cooked green peas
4 green shallots, chopped

MINT DRESSING
½ cup (125ml) oil
½ cup (125ml) cider vinegar
1 teaspoon sugar
¼ cup chopped fresh mint

Heat oil in pan, add seeds, cook, covered, until seeds start to pop. Add butter and stock, bring to boil. Stir in couscous, return to boil, remove pan from heat. Cover pan, stand about 5 minutes or until liquid is absorbed. Separate grains with fork, spread onto tray; cool at room temperature. Combine couscous, peas, shallots and mint dressing in bowl; mix lightly.
Mint Dressing: Combine all ingredients in screw-top jar; shake well.
Serves 6.

COUSCOUS, PEPPER AND ROASTED GARLIC SALAD

2 medium red peppers
12 cloves garlic, peeled
⅓ cup (80ml) olive oil
1½ cups (375ml) chicken stock
2 cups (180g) couscous
90g butter, melted

DRESSING
½ cup (125ml) tomato juice
1 tablespoon balsamic vinegar
1½ teaspoons harissa
¼ cup (60ml) olive oil
2 tablespoons chopped fresh marjoram
2 tablespoons chopped fresh chives

Quarter peppers, remove seeds and membranes. Grill peppers, skin side up, until skin blisters and blackens. Peel away skin, slice peppers finely.

Place garlic in small ovenproof dish, pour oil over garlic, bake, uncovered, in moderate oven 25 minutes or until garlic is lightly browned and tender.

Bring stock to boil in pan, stir in couscous, remove from heat, stand about 2 minutes or until liquid is absorbed. Add butter, stir over heat until couscous is coated. Spread couscous on tray, cool at room temperature. Combine couscous, peppers, roasted garlic and dressing in bowl; mix well.

Dressing: Combine all ingredients in screw-top jar; shake well.

Serves 4 to 6.

SESAME NOODLES WITH TANGY CITRUS SHREDS

375g fresh egg noodles
1 tablespoon sesame oil
1 tablespoon olive oil
2 medium oranges
2 medium limes
1 medium lemon

DRESSING
½ cup (125ml) orange juice
¼ cup (60ml) lime juice
2 tablespoons lemon juice
2 tablespoons peanut butter
1 teaspoon sambal oelek
1 tablespoon sugar
2 tablespoons cider vinegar
1 tablespoon sesame oil
1 tablespoon oil

Add noodles to large pan of boiling water, boil, uncovered until just tender; drain, rinse under cold water, drain well. Place noodles in bowl, toss with combined oils.

Using vegetable peeler, peel rind thinly from oranges, limes and lemon, avoiding any white pith; cut rind into thin shreds. Place rind in pan, cover with cold water, bring to boil; drain, rinse under cold water; drain. Combine noodle mixture, rind and dressing in bowl; mix well.

Dressing: Blend or process all ingredients until smooth.

Serves 4 to 6.

LEFT: From left: Minted Couscous with Peas and Mustard Seeds, Pasta with Beans and Tangy Onion Relish.
RIGHT: From left: Couscous, Pepper and Roasted Garlic Salad, Sesame Noodles with Tangy Citrus Shreds.

Left: Plates and tiles from Country Floors.
Right: Plates from Kenwick Galleries.

THAI SALAD WITH CRUNCHY RICE SQUARES

⅓ bunch (about 280g) bok
   choy, chopped
1 medium yellow pepper, thinly sliced
1 medium red pepper, thinly sliced
1¼ cups (about 125g) mung
   bean sprouts
2 cups (about 160g) bean sprouts
2 tablespoons shredded fresh basil

COCONUT CREAM DRESSING
½ cup (125ml) coconut cream
2 tablespoons lime juice
½ teaspoon sesame oil
½ teaspoon honey
½ teaspoon fish sauce

RICE SQUARES
1 cup (200g) white short-grain rice
2 cups (500ml) chicken stock
1 tablespoon chopped fresh basil
½ teaspoon sambal oelek
oil for deep-frying

Combine bok choy, peppers, sprouts and basil in bowl; stir in coconut cream dressing, top with rice squares.
Coconut Cream Dressing: Combine all ingredients in jar; shake well.
Rice Squares: Grease deep 15cm square cake pan, line base and sides with foil, grease foil. Combine rice and stock in pan, bring to boil, simmer, covered with tight-fitting lid, about 12 minutes or until liquid is absorbed and rice is sticky. Stir in basil and sambal oelek. Press mixture firmly into prepared pan, smooth top. Cover with greased foil, place another pan on top, weight down with heavy cans. Refrigerate several hours or overnight.

Remove rice mixture from pan, cut into 2cm squares. Deep-fry rice squares in batches in hot oil until lightly browned and crisp; drain on absorbent paper.

Serves 4 to 6.

TURTLE BEAN AND PEPPER SALAD

Turtle beans are also known as black kidney beans. Beans best prepared a day ahead.

2½ cups (525g) dried turtle beans
1 ham bone
1 small onion, halved
1 stick celery, halved
1 medium carrot, halved
3 teaspoons cumin seeds
2 medium red peppers,
   finely chopped
2 medium yellow peppers,
   finely chopped
⅓ cup chopped fresh coriander
⅓ cup chopped fresh parsley

DRESSING
½ cup (125ml) lemon juice
½ cup (125ml) olive oil
2 teaspoons Dijon mustard
1 clove garlic, crushed
½ teaspoon sugar
1 teaspoon sambal oelek

Place beans in bowl, cover well with water, cover, stand overnight.

Drain beans, discard water. Combine beans, ham bone, onion, celery and carrot in large pan, add enough water to cover mixture. Bring to boil, simmer, covered, about 1 hour or until beans are tender. Drain beans; cool. Discard water, bone and vegetables.

Place seeds in dry pan, stir over gentle heat until fragrant; cool. Combine beans, seeds, peppers and herbs in bowl, add dressing; mix well.
Dressing: Combine all ingredients in screw-top jar; shake well.

Serves 6.

HERBED POTATO AND PASTA SALAD

250g rigatoni pasta
2 large red-skinned potatoes
2 tablespoons olive oil
2 cloves garlic, crushed
1 bunch (about 650g) English spinach
1 medium radicchio lettuce
2 green shallots, chopped
¼ cup shredded fresh basil

DRESSING
2 tablespoons red wine vinegar
½ cup (125ml) olive oil
1 tablespoon Dijon mustard
3 teaspoons brown sugar

Add pasta to large pan of boiling water, boil, uncovered, until just tender; drain, rinse under cold water, drain well.

Chop potatoes into 2cm pieces. Boil, steam or microwave potatoes until tender; drain, rinse under cold water, drain well. Heat oil in pan, add garlic, spinach and torn lettuce leaves, cook, stirring, until spinach is just wilted. Combine pasta, potatoes, spinach mixture, shallots, basil and dressing in bowl; mix well. Serve warm or cold.
Dressing: Combine all ingredients in screw-top jar; shake well.

Serves 6.

LEFT: Thai Salad with Crunchy Rice Squares.
RIGHT: From left: Turtle Bean and Pepper Salad, Herbed Potato and Pasta Salad.

Left: Plate and wooden mat from Country Floors.

THREE BEAN, TOMATO AND EGGPLANT SALAD

⅓ cup (70g) dried borlotti beans
⅓ cup (70g) dried black-eyed beans
1½ cups (180g) frozen broad
    beans, thawed
1 large eggplant
2 tablespoons olive oil
2 medium tomatoes,
    seeded, chopped
1 medium red Spanish onion, sliced

DRESSING
2 tablespoons balsamic vinegar
¼ cup (60ml) olive oil
½ teaspoon grated lemon rind
2 tablespoons chopped fresh mint

Place borlotti beans and black-eyed beans in bowl, cover well with water, cover, stand overnight.

Drain beans, add to pan of boiling water, boil, uncovered, about 25 minutes or until tender; drain. Boil, steam or microwave broad beans until tender, remove outer skin.

Cut eggplant into 2cm pieces. Place

eggplant in bowl, toss with oil. Place egg-plant in single layer on oven tray, bake, uncovered, in hot oven 20 minutes, turn-ing occasionally; cool. Combine all beans, eggplant, tomatoes and onion in bowl, add dressing; mix well.
Dressing: Combine all ingredients in screw-top jar; shake well.
Serves 4.

CURRIED BROWN RICE AND CASHEW SALAD

2 cups (400g) brown rice
2 tablespoons oil
1 medium onion, finely chopped
2 cloves garlic, crushed
2 teaspoons curry powder
2 teaspoons black mustard seeds
¾ cup (120g) sultanas
¾ cup (110g) unsalted roasted
    cashews, chopped
2 medium carrots, grated
½ small red pepper, chopped
2 medium apples, peeled, grated
3 green shallots, chopped
¼ cup chopped fresh parsley

DRESSING
1 egg yolk
2 tablespoons cider vinegar
⅓ cup (80ml) oil
3 teaspoons curry powder

Add rice gradually to pan of boiling water, boil, uncovered, about 30 minutes or until tender; drain, cool.

Heat oil in pan, add onion, garlic, curry powder and seeds, cook, stirring, until onion is soft, cool. Combine rice, onion mixture, sultanas, nuts, carrots, pepper, apples, shallots and half the parsley in bowl, add dressing; mix well. Sprinkle with remaining parsley.
Dressing: Blend or process all ingre-dients until smooth.

Serves 8.

CURRIED PASTA AND RADISH SALAD

3 cups (250g) shell pasta
4 green shallots, chopped
10 radishes, sliced

CURRIED MAYONNAISE
1 tablespoon oil
1 tablespoon curry powder
1 tablespoon seeded mustard
1 tablespoon chopped fresh chives
½ cup (60g) grated tasty cheese
1½ cups (375ml) mayonnaise
2 tablespoons milk

Add pasta to large pan of boiling water, boil, uncovered, until just tender; drain, rinse under cold water, drain well. Combine pasta, shallots and radishes in bowl, add curried mayonnaise; mix well.
Curried Mayonnaise: Heat oil in pan, add curry powder, cook, stirring, until fragrant; cool. Combine curry mixture with remaining ingredients in bowl; mix well.

Serves 4 to 6.

MINTED RICE WITH FETA CHEESE

⅓ cup (80ml) olive oil
1 medium onion, finely chopped
2 cups (400g) white long-grain rice
3 cups (750ml) chicken stock
150g feta cheese, crumbled
½ cup chopped fresh mint

Heat oil in pan, add onion, cook, stirring, until soft. Add rice gradually, cook, stirring, 1 minute. Add stock, bring to boil, cook, covered, over low heat about 20 minutes or until liquid is absorbed and rice is tender. Remove pan from heat, stir in cheese and mint; cool. Spoon rice into 6 lightly oiled moulds (1 cup/250ml capacity), cover, refrigerate several hours or overnight. Turn out to serve.

Serves 6.

LEFT: From left: Three Bean, Tomato and Eggplant Salad, Curried Brown Rice and Cashew Salad.
RIGHT: From top: Curried Pasta and Radish Salad, Minted Rice with Feta Cheese.

Left: Plate from Butler & Co. Right: Tray, china and wooden servers from The Bay Tree.

SPICY RICE WITH CRISP ONION AND COCONUT

pinch ground saffron
2 star anise
1 cinnamon stick
3 cardamom pods, crushed
2½ cups (500g) basmati rice
¼ cup (35g) slivered
    almonds, toasted
½ cup (25g) flaked coconut, toasted
4 green shallots, chopped
1 small onion, thinly sliced
oil for deep-frying

COCONUT DRESSING
1⅔ cups (410ml) coconut cream
2 tablespoons lime juice
1 teaspoon sugar
½ teaspoon garam masala

Add saffron, star anise, cinnamon and cardamom to large pan of cold water, bring to boil, add rice gradually, boil, un-covered, until tender; drain. Discard star anise and cinnamon stick, rinse rice under cold water; drain well. Combine rice, nuts, coconut, shallots and coconut dressing in bowl; mix well.

Deep-fry onion in hot oil until lightly browned; drain on absorbent paper. Sprinkle onion over salad.
Coconut Dressing: Combine all ingredients in bowl; mix well.

Serves 4 to 6.

CRUNCHY TOMATO AND FETTUCCINE SALAD

250g spinach fettuccine pasta
3 slices wholemeal bread
2 cloves garlic, crushed
1 tablespoon olive oil
250g cherry tomatoes, halved
⅓ cup shredded fresh basil
⅓ cup (25g) parmesan cheese flakes

DRESSING
1 cup firmly packed fresh basil leaves
2 cloves garlic, crushed
⅓ cup (45g) drained chopped
    sun-dried tomatoes
½ cup (125ml) olive oil
¼ cup (60ml) balsamic vinegar
1 teaspoon sugar
¼ teaspoon dried chilli flakes

Add pasta to large pan of boiling water, boil, uncovered, until just tender; drain, rinse under cold water, drain well.

Process bread until finely crumbed, add garlic, process until combined. Heat oil in pan, add breadcrumb mixture, stir over heat until breadcrumbs are browned and crisp. Combine pasta, tomatoes, basil and dressing in bowl; mix well. Sprinkle with breadcrumbs and cheese.
Dressing: Blend or process all ingredients until combined.

Serves 6.

CHERRY TOMATO AND SPINACH RAVIOLI SALAD

500g spinach and ricotta ravioli
200g snow peas
1 medium red pepper, sliced
250g cherry tomatoes
4 green shallots, chopped
½ medium red Spanish onion, sliced

CREAMY HERB DRESSING
⅓ cup (80ml) olive oil
2 tablespoons white vinegar
½ cup (125ml) sour cream
1 clove garlic, crushed
1 tablespoon chopped fresh chives
2 teaspoons chopped fresh thyme
2 teaspoons chopped fresh rosemary
2 teaspoons chopped fresh basil

Add pasta to large pan of boiling water, boil, uncovered, until just tender; drain, cool. Boil, steam or microwave snow peas until just tender; drain, rinse under cold water, drain well.

Combine pasta, snow peas, pepper, tomatoes, shallots and onion in bowl; add creamy herb dressing.
Creamy Herb Dressing: Combine all ingredients in screw-top jar; shake well.

Serves 8.

CRACKED WHEAT AND RICE SALAD

½ cup (40g) burghul
1¼ cups (250g) white rice
½ cup (100g) wild rice
425g can baby corn, drained
4 green shallots, chopped

DRESSING
2 tablespoons light soy sauce
¼ teaspoon sesame oil
2 tablespoons honey
⅓ cup (80ml) oil
1 clove garlic, crushed

Place burghul in bowl, cover with boiling water, stand 15 minutes. Rinse burghul, drain, pat dry with absorbent paper. Add rices gradually to separate pans of boiling water, boil, uncovered, until just tender; drain, rinse under cold water, drain well.

Combine burghul, rices, corn and shallots in bowl. Add dressing, mix gently; cover, refrigerate 1 hour.
Dressing: Combine all ingredients in screw-top jar; shake well.

Serves 6.

LEFT: From left: Crunchy Tomato and Fettuccine Salad, Spicy Rice with Crisp Onion and Coconut.
RIGHT: From back: Cracked Wheat and Rice Salad, Cherry Tomato and Spinach Ravioli Salad.

Left: Plates and tiles from Country Floors.
Right: Plates from The Bay Tree; tiles from Country Floors.

DEEP-FRIED PASTA SALAD

2 cups (150g) farfalle pasta
plain flour
3 eggs, lightly beaten
¼ cup (60ml) milk
2½ cups (175g) stale breadcrumbs
1 cup (80g) grated parmesan cheese
oil for deep-frying

HERB DRESSING
¼ cup (60ml) lemon juice
¼ cup (60ml) bottled Italian dressing
2 cups (500ml) olive oil
1 tablespoon chopped fresh mint
1 tablespoon chopped fresh thyme
1 tablespoon chopped
fresh rosemary

Add pasta to large pan of boiling water, boil, uncovered, until tender; drain, pat dry on absorbent paper. Toss pasta in flour, shake away excess flour. Dip pasta in combined eggs and milk, toss in combined breadcrumbs and cheese. Cover pasta, refrigerate 1 hour.

Deep-fry pasta in batches in hot oil until lightly browned and crisp; drain on absorbent paper. Serve pasta hot or cold; drizzle with herb dressing.
Herb Dressing: Combine all ingredients in screw-top jar; shake well.

Serves 4.

FRUITY RICE AND CASHEW SALAD

2 cups (400g) brown rice
½ cup (75g) chopped dried pears
½ cup (45g) chopped dried apricots
¼ cup (35g) chopped dried peaches
½ cup (80g) sultanas
½ cup (75g) unsalted roasted cashews
4 green shallots, chopped

DRESSING
1 tablespoon grated fresh ginger
2 tablespoons chopped fresh mint
1 cup (250ml) apricot nectar
¼ teaspoon ground cardamom
1 tablespoon lemon juice

Add rice gradually to large pan of boiling water, boil, uncovered, about 30 minutes or until tender; drain, rinse under cold water, drain well.

Combine rice, fruit, nuts and shallots in bowl, add dressing; mix well.
Dressing: Combine all ingredients in screw-top jar; shake well.

Serves 4 to 6.

WILD RICE AND BARLEY SALAD WITH PISTACHIOS

¼ cup (50g) wild rice
½ cup (50g) pearl barley
1 medium lime
1 medium grapefruit
½ cup (75g) unsalted
   pistachios, toasted
2 tablespoons sesame seeds, toasted
2 tablespoons pepitas
2 tablespoons sunflower seed kernels
5 dried pears, sliced
6 prunes, sliced
1 tablespoon lime juice
2 teaspoons honey
½ teaspoon sesame oil

LEFT: From back: Fruity Rice and Cashew Salad, Deep-Fried Pasta Salad.
ABOVE: From left: Wild Rice and Barley Salad with Pistachios, Caesar Pasta Salad.

Left : China from Primex Products Pty Ltd.
Above: Plates from H.A.G. Imports, tiles from Country Floors.

Add rice and barley gradually to pan of boiling water, boil, uncovered, stirring occasionally, about 30 minutes or until tender; drain, rinse under cold water, drain.

Using vegetable peeler, peel rind thinly from lime and grapefruit, avoiding any white pith. Cut rind into thin strips. Add rind to pan of boiling water, boil 1 minute; drain, rinse under cold water, drain. Combine rice, barley, rind, segmented grapefruit and remaining ingredients in bowl; mix well.

Serves 2 to 4.

CAESAR PASTA SALAD

250g spiral pasta
1 teaspoon olive oil
1 medium cos lettuce
56g can anchovy fillets, drained,
   chopped
½ cup (40g) parmesan cheese flakes

DRESSING
6 green shallots, chopped
3 cloves garlic, crushed
½ cup (125ml) olive oil
2 tablespoons lemon juice
1 egg white
1 teaspoon Dijon mustard

GARLIC CROUTONS
1 small French bread stick
50g butter, melted
2 cloves garlic, crushed

Add pasta to large pan of boiling water, boil, uncovered, until just tender; drain, rinse under cold water, drain well. Place pasta in bowl; toss with oil.

Combine torn lettuce leaves, pasta, anchovies and half the cheese in bowl, add dressing; mix well. Add garlic croutons, sprinkle with remaining cheese.
Dressing: Blend or process all ingredients until well combined.
Garlic Croutons: Cut bread into 2cm slices, cut slices into quarters. Toss bread in combined butter and garlic. Bake croutons on oven tray in moderate oven about 15 minutes or until crisp.

Serves 4.

LASAGNETTE WITH MANGOES AND RAISINS

250g lasagnette pasta
1 tablespoon olive oil
¼ teaspoon ground cloves
¼ teaspoon ground cardamom
¼ teaspoon ground cumin
1 teaspoon paprika
1 medium onion, chopped
2 cloves garlic, crushed
2 small mangoes, chopped
⅔ cup (110g) raisins
2 tablespoons chopped fresh chives
¼ cup chopped fresh parsley
⅓ cup (80ml) olive oil, extra
1 tablespoon white vinegar

Add pasta to large pan of boiling water, boil, uncovered, until just tender; drain, rinse under cold water, drain well.

Heat oil in pan, add spices, onion and garlic, cook, stirring, until onion is soft, cool. Combine pasta, onion mixture and remaining ingredients in bowl; mix well.

Serves 6.

LENTIL SALAD WITH BLUE CHEESE DRESSING

1 small green pepper
1 small red pepper
1 large carrot
½ small leek
½ cup (100g) red lentils
½ cup (100g) brown lentils
15 slices hot salami

BLUE CHEESE DRESSING
30g blue cheese
½ cup (125ml) thickened cream
2 teaspoons sour cream
1 teaspoon lemon juice
2 teaspoons chopped fresh dill

Remove seeds and membranes from peppers. Cut peppers, carrot and leek into very thin strips about the same size. Place vegetables in bowl, cover with iced water, stand about 20 minutes or until vegetables curl slightly; drain well.

Add red lentils to pan of boiling water, simmer, uncovered, about 8 minutes or until tender; drain, cool.

Add brown lentils to pan of boiling water, simmer, uncovered, about 20 minutes or until tender; drain, cool.

Cut salami into thin strips. Combine vegetables, lentils and salami in bowl; top with blue cheese dressing.

Blue Cheese Dressing: Combine crumbled cheese with remaining ingredients in bowl; beat until well combined.

Serves 4 to 6.

PROSCIUTTO AND BEAN SALAD WITH CHIVE DRESSING

100g sliced prosciutto
1 medium bunch curly endive
1 medium cos lettuce
2 x 310g cans butter beans, rinsed, drained

CHIVE DRESSING
¼ cup (60ml) sherry wine vinegar
1 teaspoon Dijon mustard
½ cup (125ml) olive oil
2 teaspoons sugar
2 tablespoons chopped fresh chives

Cut prosciutto into thin strips, combine with torn endive and lettuce leaves and beans in bowl; drizzle with chive dressing.
Chive Dressing: Combine all ingredients in screw-top jar; shake well.

Serves 4 to 6.

CORIANDER, LENTIL AND VEGETABLE SALAD

⅔ cup (130g) red lentils
1 medium carrot
1 small red pepper
1 cup (about 80g) shredded Chinese cabbage
4 cups (about 320g) bean sprouts

CORIANDER DRESSING
1 cup firmly packed coriander leaves
2 cloves garlic, crushed
½ teaspoon sambal oelek
⅔ cup (160ml) olive oil
1 tablespoon light soy sauce

Add lentils to pan of boiling water, simmer, uncovered, about 8 minutes or until lentils are just tender; drain, rinse under cold water, drain well. Cut carrot and pepper into very thin matchsticks.

Combine lentils, carrot, pepper, cabbage and sprouts in bowl; mix well, top with coriander dressing.
Coriander Dressing: Blend or process all ingredients until smooth.

Serves 6.

LEFT: From top: Lentil Salad with Blue Cheese Dressing, Lasagnette with Mangoes and Raisins.
RIGHT: From back: Coriander, Lentil and Vegetable Salad, Prosciutto and Bean Salad with Chive Dressing.

Left: Glassware by Julio Santos, available from Australian Craftworks.
Right: Tray and bowls from The Bay Tree.

SWEET POTATO AND CHICK PEA SALAD

300g kumara
300g white sweet potato
⅓ cup (80ml) oil
30g butter
1 medium onion, chopped
¼ teaspoon chilli powder
¼ teaspoon ground cinnamon
1 cup (125g) cooked peas
310g can chick peas, rinsed, drained

Cut kumara and sweet potato into 3cm pieces. Heat oil and butter in pan, add onion, cook, stirring, until soft. Add kumara and sweet potato, cook slowly, covered, stirring occasionally, until vegetables are tender. Add spices, peas and chick peas, cook, stirring, until heated through. Serve warm or cold.

Serves 4.

CORN AND BLACK-EYED BEAN SALAD

1 cup (200g) dried black-eyed beans
2 medium green peppers
1 tablespoon cumin seeds
440g can corn kernels, rinsed, drained
250g cherry tomatoes
4 green shallots, chopped
2 tablespoons chopped fresh coriander

DRESSING
¼ cup (60ml) sherry wine vinegar
½ cup (125ml) olive oil
2 teaspoons sugar

Place beans in bowl, cover with boiling water, stand 1 hour. Drain beans, add to pan of boiling water, simmer, partly covered, about 30 minutes or until tender; drain, rinse under cold water, drain well.

Quarter peppers, remove seeds and membranes. Grill peppers, skin side up, on oven tray until skin blisters and blackens. Peel away skin, cut peppers into strips. Add seeds to dry pan, stir over heat until fragrant. Combine beans, peppers, seeds, corn, tomatoes, shallots and coriander in bowl; add dressing, mix gently. Refrigerate until cold.

Dressing; Combine all ingredients in screw-top jar; shake well.

Serves 6.

BELOW: From left: Sweet Potato and Chick Pea Salad, Corn and Black-Eyed Bean Salad.
RIGHT: From left: Pumpkin, Rice and Seed Salad, Curried Chick Pea Salad.

Below: Wooden mat from Country Floors.

PUMPKIN, RICE AND SEED SALAD

1 cup (200g) white rice
3 green shallots, chopped
¼ cup (35g) sesame seeds, toasted
¼ cup (40g) sunflower seed kernels
¼ cup (40g) pepitas
100g uncooked pumpkin,
   coarsely grated

DRESSING
2 tablespoons white vinegar
2 tablespoons honey
1 tablespoon light soy sauce
½ cup (125ml) oil
2 tablespoons green ginger wine
pinch ground saffron

Add rice gradually to pan of boiling water,
boil, uncovered, until tender; drain, rinse
under cold water, drain well. Combine rice
with remaining ingredients in bowl, add
dressing; mix well.
Dressing: Combine all ingredients in
screw-top jar; shake well.
Serves 4.

CURRIED CHICK PEA SALAD

3 x 310g cans chick peas,
   rinsed, drained
1 small red Spanish onion,
   finely chopped
1 large mango, finely chopped
1 medium apple, peeled, chopped
1 tablespoon chopped fresh mint
1 tablespoon chopped
   fresh coriander
¼ cup (15g) shredded
   coconut, toasted

DRESSING
¾ cup (180 ml) plain yogurt
3 teaspoons mango chutney
1 clove garlic, crushed
2 teaspoons curry powder
1 tablespoon lime juice

Combine all ingredients and dressing in
bowl; mix well.
Dressing: Combine all ingredients in
bowl; mix well.
Serves 4 to 6.

EGGPLANT, TOMATO AND ZUCCHINI STACKS

1 large (about 500g) eggplant
oil for deep-frying
2 medium zucchini, thinly sliced
1 medium yellow pepper
2 large tomatoes

PESTO
1 cup firmly packed fresh basil leaves
1 clove garlic, crushed
¼ cup (40g) pine nuts, toasted
⅓ cup (80ml) olive oil
¼ cup (20g) grated parmesan cheese

DRESSING
½ cup (125ml) olive oil
1 tablespoon balsamic vinegar
¼ teaspoon sugar
1 clove garlic, crushed

Cut eggplant into 12 x 1cm slices. Deep-fry eggplant in batches in hot oil until lightly browned; drain on absorbent paper. Deep-fry zucchini in batches in hot oil until just tender; drain on absorbent paper.

Quarter pepper, remove seeds and membrane. Grill pepper, skin side up, until skin blisters and blackens. Peel away skin, cut pepper into thin strips. Slice tomatoes into 8 x 1cm slices.

Spread eggplant slices thickly with pesto. Place 4 of the largest eggplant slices on plates, top with zucchini slices, half the tomato slices, another 4 medium eggplant slices, pepper strips, remaining tomato slices then remaining eggplant slices. Drizzle with dressing, cover, refrigerate 2 hours. Decorate with extra pepper strips, if desired.

Pesto: Blend or process basil, garlic, nuts and oil until smooth; stir in cheese.

Dressing: Combine all ingredients in screw-top jar; shake well.

Serves 4.

VEGETABLE NESTS WITH MUSTARD DRESSING

1 medium leek
1 large carrot
2 large zucchini
1 tablespoon fresh lemon thyme leaves

MUSTARD DRESSING
20g butter
2 teaspoons mustard seeds
½ cup (125ml) dry white wine
½ cup (125ml) cream
2 teaspoons seeded mustard

Cut leek into 2cm x 24cm strips. Using a vegetable peeler, peel strips lengthways from carrot and zucchini. Add vegetable strips to pan of boiling water, bring to boil; drain immediately, rinse under cold water, drain on absorbent paper. Take 2 strips of each vegetable, twist into a nest, place on plate. Repeat with remaining vegetable strips. Sprinkle nests with thyme; drizzle with mustard dressing.

Mustard Dressing: Heat butter in pan, add seeds, cook, covered, until seeds pop. Add wine, cream and mustard, simmer, uncovered, until thickened slightly.

Serves 4 to 6.

ORIENTAL CUCUMBER SALAD

3 small green cucumbers, thinly sliced
coarse cooking salt
2 small fresh red chillies,
**   finely chopped**
¼ cup (60ml) rice vinegar
1 tablespoon sesame oil
1 tablespoon olive oil
1 tablespoon light soy sauce
2 teaspoons sugar
2 tablespoons mirin
2 teaspoons grated fresh ginger

Sprinkle cucumbers with salt, cover, refrigerate 1 hour. Rinse cucumbers under cold water, pat dry with absorbent paper. Combine cucumbers with remaining ingredients in bowl; mix well. Cover, refrigerate 10 minutes. Drain cucumbers and serve; discard marinade.

Serves 4.

LEFT: Clockwise from left: Vegetable Nests with Mustard Dressing, Eggplant, Tomato and Zucchini Stacks, Oriental Cucumber Salad.
ABOVE: Barbecued Vegetable Salad.

Left: Plates from Albi Imports; wooden bowl from Accoutrement.
Above: Glass plate from The Melbourne Shop.

BARBECUED VEGETABLE SALAD

1 medium eggplant
3 medium zucchini
coarse cooking salt
300g pumpkin
1 large onion
1 medium red pepper, quartered
olive oil

DRESSING
2 tablespoons lemon juice
½ cup (125ml) olive oil
¼ teaspoon sugar
2 teaspoons drained green
**   peppercorns, crushed**
1 tablespoon drained small capers
1 clove garlic, crushed

Slice eggplant and zucchini lengthways into 5mm slices. Sprinkle with salt, stand 30 minutes.

Rinse eggplant and zucchini under cold water, drain on absorbent paper. Cut pumpkin and onion into 5mm slices. Cut pepper into 2cm strips. Brush vegetables with oil, barbecue on both sides until browned. Combine vegetables on plate, top with dressing.

Dressing: Combine all ingredients in screw-top jar; shake well.

Serves 4 to 6.

TURNIP AND FENNEL SALAD

1 medium white turnip
1 medium fennel bulb, thinly sliced
2 tablespoons pepitas, toasted
¼ cup (35g) slivered almonds, toasted

VINAIGRETTE
¼ cup (60ml) olive oil
2 tablespoons cider vinegar
1 teaspoon seasoned pepper
2 tablespoons chopped fresh parsley

Peel turnip, cut into thin strips. Boil, steam or microwave turnip until just tender; drain, rinse under cold water, drain. Combine turnip, fennel, pepitas and nuts in bowl, add vinaigrette; mix well.
Vinaigrette: Combine all ingredients in screw-top jar; shake well.

Serves 4.

BELOW: From top: Turnip and Fennel Salad, Marinated Bocconcini and Tomato Salad.

Below: Glass plates and bowl from Amy's Tableware.

MARINATED BOCCONCINI AND TOMATO SALAD

Bocconcini best marinated a day ahead; store, covered, in refrigerator.

¼ cup (60ml) olive oil
2 teaspoons chopped fresh mint
2 tablespoons firmly packed fresh basil leaves
2 teaspoons lemon juice
2 teaspoons balsamic vinegar
4 (about 90g) bocconcini
2 large tomatoes, sliced

DRESSING
¾ cup (180ml) olive oil
2 teaspoons chopped fresh mint
¼ cup firmly packed fresh basil leaves
½ teaspoon grated lemon rind
3 teaspoons lemon juice

Blend or process oil, herbs, juice and vinegar until smooth. Combine basil mixture and bocconcini in bowl, cover, refrigerate overnight. Remove bocconcini from marinade, discard marinade, cut bocconcini into 5mm slices. Serve bocconcini with tomatoes; top with dressing.
Dressing: Blend or process all ingredients until smooth.

Serves 4.

ZUCCHINI, CUCUMBER AND FENNEL SALAD

2 small green cucumbers, peeled, seeded
4 medium zucchini
1 medium grapefruit
30g butter
2 teaspoons fennel seeds
½ teaspoon sugar
2 teaspoons chopped fresh thyme
1 tablespoon grapefruit juice
1 tablespoon white wine vinegar
2 teaspoons olive oil

Cut cucumbers and zucchini into matchsticks. Using a vegetable peeler, peel rind thinly from grapefruit, avoiding any white pith; cut rind into thin strips.

Heat butter in pan, add zucchini, rind and seeds, cook, stirring, until zucchini are just tender. Strain butter from zucchini mixture; reserve butter. Combine zucchini mixture and cucumber in bowl.

Heat reserved butter in pan, add remaining ingredients, simmer, uncovered, until reduced by half. Top zucchini mixture with butter mixture.

Serves 4.

MIXED VEGETABLE SALAD WITH YOGURT DRESSING

2 sticks celery, chopped
2 medium tomatoes, chopped
½ cup (60g) cooked green peas
6 medium radishes, chopped
1 medium red pepper, chopped
**2 small green cucumbers,
    seeded, chopped**

YOGURT DRESSING
1 teaspoon ground cumin
1 teaspoon ground fennel
½ teaspoon seasoned pepper
1 cup (250ml) plain yogurt

Combine all ingredients in bowl; add yogurt dressing, mix well.
Yogurt Dressing: Add spices to dry pan, stir over heat until fragrant. Combine spice mixture with yogurt in bowl; whisk until smooth.
Serves 6.

CELERIAC AND CARROT SALAD WITH CAPERS

1 medium (about 630g) celeriac
2 tablespoons white vinegar
3 cups (750ml) water
2 medium carrots
200g sliced ham
2 tablespoons drained capers

DRESSING
¼ cup (60ml) sour cream
⅓ cup (80ml) mayonnaise
1 tablespoon grated lemon rind
2 tablespoons lemon juice

Peel and cut celeriac into thin strips, place in bowl, cover with combined vinegar and water. Cut carrots and ham into thin strips. Drain celeriac; dry on absorbent paper. Combine celeriac, carrots, ham and capers in bowl, add dressing; mix well.
Dressing: Combine all ingredients in bowl; whisk well.
Serves 6.

WARM CAULIFLOWER WITH CHILLI GARLIC DRESSING

750g cauliflower, chopped
½ cup (80g) sunflower seed kernels
2 tablespoons chopped fresh chives

CHILLI GARLIC DRESSING
½ cup (125ml) olive oil
3 teaspoons sweet chilli sauce
2 tablespoons red wine vinegar
3 cloves garlic, crushed

Boil, steam or microwave cauliflower until just tender; drain, rinse under cold water, drain. Combine cauliflower, seeds and chives in bowl, add chilli garlic dressing; mix lightly. Serve warm or cold.
Chilli Garlic Dressing: Combine all ingredients in screw-top jar; shake well.
Serves 4.

ABOVE: From top: Warm Cauliflower with Chilli Garlic Dressing, Zucchini, Cucumber and Fennel Salad.
RIGHT: From left: Celeriac and Carrot Salad with Capers, Mixed Vegetable Salad with Yogurt Dressing.

Above: Bowls from Amy's Tableware.

FILLO BASKETS WITH GREEN VEGETABLES AND GINGER

2 sheets fillo pastry
oil for deep-frying
50g piece fresh ginger
50g green beans, sliced
75g snow peas
75g sugar snap peas
2 green shallots
½ cup (75g) unsalted roasted cashews
40g snow pea sprouts

LEMON GINGER DRESSING
1 teaspoon grated fresh ginger
2 cloves garlic, crushed
2 tablespoons lemon juice
½ teaspoon sesame oil
½ teaspoon fish sauce
2 tablespoons oil
¼ teaspoon light soy sauce

Cut both sheets of pastry in half crossways, cut each half into 4. Layer 4 pieces of pastry over inside of lightly oiled double strainer. Press top of strainer onto pastry. Lower strainer into hot oil, holding handles firmly together, deep-fry until pastry is lightly browned; drain basket on absorbent paper. Repeat with remaining pastry.

Peel and slice ginger lengthways, cut each slice into thin strips. Deep-fry ginger in batches in hot oil until lightly browned; drain on absorbent paper.

Boil, steam or microwave beans and both peas until just tender; drain, rinse under cold water, drain. Cut shallots into 6cm lengths. Combine beans, peas, shallots, nuts and sprouts in bowl. Fill baskets with vegetable mixture, top with lemon ginger dressing and fried ginger.
Lemon Ginger Dressing: Blend or process all ingredients until smooth.

Serves 4.

FRESH BEETROOT AND WATERCRESS SALAD

8 (about 1.2kg) fresh beetroot
3 cups (about 150g) firmly packed watercress sprigs

DRESSING
⅓ cup (80ml) white wine vinegar
½ cup (125ml) walnut oil
¼ cup (60ml) oil
1 teaspoon Dijon mustard
2 cloves garlic, crushed

Boil, steam or microwave beetroot until just tender; drain, rinse under cold water, drain. Peel beetroot, cut into quarters. Combine beetroot and dressing in bowl, cover, refrigerate 1 hour. Add watercress to beetroot mixture; mix gently.
Dressing: Combine all ingredients in screw-top jar; shake well.

Serves 4 to 6.

ORANGE AND GREEN VEGETABLE SALAD

½ bunch (about 125g) fresh asparagus spears, chopped
200g broccoli, chopped
150g snow peas
150g sugar snap peas
1 small green cucumber, seeded, sliced
1 medium orange, segmented
1 tablespoon chopped roasted hazelnuts

DRESSING
⅓ cup (80ml) oil
1 tablespoon hazelnut oil
2 tablespoons red wine vinegar
1 tablespoon orange juice
½ teaspoon seeded mustard
½ teaspoon sugar

Boil, steam or microwave asparagus, broccoli and both peas until just tender; drain, rinse under cold water, drain. Combine vegetables, cucumber and dressing in bowl; mix well. Top with orange segments and nuts.
Dressing: Combine all ingredients in screw-top jar; shake well.

Serves 4.

CRUDITES WITH TWO DIPS

½ medium red pepper
½ medium yellow pepper
½ bunch (about 10) radishes
1 bunch (about 12) baby carrots
60g snow peas
100g cherry tomatoes
12 quail eggs, hard-boiled

EGGPLANT DIP
2 small eggplants
1 tablespoon oil
2 cloves garlic, crushed
1 tablespoon lemon juice

2 tablespoons oil, extra
¼ teaspoon sambal oelek
2 tablespoons chopped fresh basil
1 tablespoon chopped fresh mint

CARROT DIP
2 large carrots, chopped
1 cup (250ml) water
1 vegetable stock cube
1 clove garlic, crushed
¼ teaspoon ground cumin
¼ teaspoon ground coriander
2 teaspoons sherry vinegar
2 tablespoons olive oil

Cut peppers into thin strips. Serve peppers, radishes, carrots, peas, tomatoes and eggs with eggplant and carrot dips.
Eggplant Dip: Halve eggplants lengthways, make diagonal cuts on cut side, place on oven tray, brush with oil. Bake, uncovered, in moderate oven about 1¼ hours or until very tender; cool. Scoop out flesh, discard skin. Blend or process eggplants, garlic, juice, extra oil and sambal oelek until smooth, stir in herbs.
Carrot Dip: Combine carrots, water and crumbled stock cube in pan, simmer, covered, until carrots are very tender; drain. Process carrots with remaining ingredients until smooth.

Serves 4.

LEFT: Clockwise from back: Orange and Green Vegetable Salad, Fresh Beetroot and Watercress Salad, Fillo Baskets with Green Vegetables and Ginger.
BELOW: Crudites with Two Dips.

Left: Tiles from Country Floors; salad servers from Corso de Fiori.

Below: Plate from Corso de Fiori.

MUSHROOM AND ARTICHOKE SALAD

12 drained artichoke hearts
½ teaspoon coriander seeds, crushed
½ teaspoon cumin seeds
250g baby mushrooms, quartered
½ cup (about 50g) mung bean sprouts
1 tablespoon chopped fresh parsley
1 tablespoon chopped fresh chives

DRESSING
⅓ cup (80ml) virgin olive oil
2 tablespoons raspberry vinegar
½ teaspoon sugar

Cut artichokes in half. Combine seeds in dry pan, cook, stirring, until fragrant; cool. Combine artichokes, seed mixture, mushrooms, sprouts, herbs and dressing in bowl; mix well.
Dressing: Combine all ingredients in screw-top jar; shake well.

Serves 4.

GRATED PUMPKIN AND ZUCCHINI SALAD

2 medium zucchini, grated
300g pumpkin, grated
2 tablespoons sesame seeds, toasted

DRESSING
¼ cup (60ml) mayonnaise
1 tablespoon water
1 teaspoon honey
1½ teaspoons grated fresh ginger

CHEESY CROUTONS
1 torpedo roll
40g butter, melted
⅓ cup (25g) finely grated parmesan cheese
½ teaspoon paprika

Combine zucchini, pumpkin and seeds in bowl, add dressing; mix lightly. Serve with cheesy croutons.
Dressing: Combine all ingredients in screw-top jar; shake well.
Cheesy Croutons: Thinly slice roll diagonally to form croutons. Brush both sides of croutons with butter, place on oven tray. Bake in moderate oven about 15 minutes or until lightly browned. Toss croutons in combined cheese and paprika. Place croutons on oven tray, sprinkle with any remaining cheese mixture, bake further 2 minutes; cool.

Serves 4.

ROASTED PEPPER SALAD

2 medium red peppers
2 medium yellow peppers
2 medium green peppers
¼ cup (40g) pine nuts, toasted
4 anchovy fillets, thinly sliced
16 baby black olives

DRESSING
1 tablespoon balsamic vinegar
2 cloves garlic, crushed
¼ cup (60ml) olive oil
1 tablespoon chopped fresh oregano

Quarter peppers, remove seeds and membranes. Grill peppers, skin side up, until skin blisters and blackens. Peel away skin. Place peppers on plate, drizzle with dressing, sprinkle with nuts, anchovies and olives.
Dressing: Combine all ingredients in screw-top jar; shake well.

Serves 4 to 6.

HERBED CORN SALAD

425g can young corn spears, drained
440g can corn kernels, drained
2 green shallots, chopped

DRESSING
¼ cup (60ml) oil
1 tablespoon cider vinegar
2 teaspoons chopped fresh chives
2 teaspoons chopped fresh basil
1 teaspoon chopped fresh thyme
¼ teaspoon sugar

Cut corn spears into 2cm lengths. Combine corn spears, corn kernels, shallots and dressing in bowl; mix well.
Dressing: Combine all ingredients in screw-top jar: shake well.

Serves 4.

LEFT: From left: Mushroom and Artichoke Salad, Grated Pumpkin and Zucchini Salad. BELOW: From left: Herbed Corn Salad, Roasted Pepper Salad.

Left: Plates from Corso de Fiori; tiles from Country Floors.

Below: Large serving platter from Albi Imports.

GAZPACHO SALAD

2 small green cucumbers, chopped
4 green shallots, chopped
4 medium tomatoes, chopped
2 medium red peppers, chopped

DRESSING
1 green shallot, chopped
¼ cup (60ml) V8 vegetable juice
2 tablespoons olive oil
1 tablespoon red wine vinegar
½ teaspoon sugar

Combine all ingredients in bowl; mix well, stir in dressing.
Dressing: Combine all ingredients in screw-top jar; shake well.

Serves 6 to 8.

BAKED VEGETABLES WITH CARDAMOM SYRUP

2 large parsnips
600g kumara
1 tablespoon oil

CARDAMOM SYRUP
1 medium lime
1 tablespoon lime juice
¼ cup (55g) sugar
¼ cup (60ml) water
¼ cup (60ml) white vinegar
½ teaspoon cardamom seeds
½ small fresh red chilli, finely chopped
2 cloves garlic, thinly sliced
1 tablespoon redcurrant jelly

Peel and cut parsnips and kumara into 3cm pieces. Place parsnips and kumara into baking dish, drizzle with oil. Bake, uncovered, in moderately hot oven about 25 minutes or until vegetables are tender, stirring occasionally; cool. Top parsnips and kumara with cardamom syrup.
Cardamom Syrup: Using a vegetable peeler, peel rind thinly from lime, avoiding any white pith; cut rind into thin strips. Combine rind with remaining ingredients in pan, stir over heat, without boiling, until sugar is dissolved and jelly melted, then simmer, uncovered, 2 minutes; cool.

Serves 4.

BEETROOT CABBAGE SALAD

1 teaspoon caraway seeds
850g can whole baby beets, drained
¼ medium cabbage, shredded

DRESSING
2 tablespoons cider vinegar
1 teaspoon Dijon mustard
1 teaspoon grated orange rind
1 teaspoon honey
½ cup (125ml) olive oil

Add seeds to pan, stir over heat until fragrant. Cut beets into strips, combine with cabbage and dressing in bowl; add seeds.
Dressing: Combine all ingredients in screw-top jar; shake well.

Serves 6.

MARINATED LEEKS

4 medium leeks
1 tablespoon chopped fresh chives

DRESSING
1 clove garlic, crushed
½ cup (125ml) olive oil
¼ cup (60ml) balsamic vinegar
1 tablespoon Dijon mustard
1 green shallot, finely chopped
1 teaspoon seasoned pepper

Using only white parts of leeks, cut leeks lengthways into quarters. Steam or microwave leeks until tender; drain, pat dry with absorbent paper. Pour dressing over warm leeks; cover, stand at room temperature 2 hours. Serve marinated leeks sprinkled with chives.
Dressing: Combine all ingredients in screw-top jar; shake well.

Serves 4 to 6.

MINTED RED CABBAGE AND ORANGE SALAD

250g sugar snap peas
½ small red cabbage, shredded
2 large oranges, segmented

MINTY ORANGE DRESSING
½ cup (125ml) orange juice
1 tablespoon chopped fresh mint
1 tablespoon white vinegar
¼ cup (60ml) oil

Boil, steam or microwave peas until just tender; drain, rinse under cold water, drain well. Combine peas, cabbage and oranges in bowl, add minty orange dressing; mix lightly.
Minty Orange Dressing: Combine all ingredients in screw-top jar; shake well.

Serves 4 to 6.

LEFT: Clockwise from left: Beetroot Cabbage Salad, Baked Vegetables with Cardamom Syrup, Gazpacho Salad.
ABOVE: From top: Marinated Leeks, Minted Red Cabbage and Orange Salad.

Left: China from Opus Design.
Above: Green glass platter by Keith Rowe from Australian Craftworks.

WINTER VEGETABLES WITH GARLIC MAYONNAISE

1 medium carrot
1 medium parsnip
1 medium leek
150g kumara
250g Jerusalem artichokes
1 small (about 450g) celeriac
¼ cup (60ml) lemon juice
4 baby new potatoes
¼ cup (60ml) dry white wine
¼ cup (60ml) olive oil
1 tablespoon chopped fresh thyme
1 tablespoon chopped fresh rosemary

GARLIC MAYONNAISE
1 egg
1 egg yolk
½ teaspoon French mustard
1 tablespoon lemon juice
2 cloves garlic, crushed
1 cup (250ml) olive oil
1 tablespoon chopped fresh chives

Cut carrot, parsnip, leek, kumara, artichokes and celeriac lengthways into wedges. Add celeriac and juice to pan of boiling water, simmer until tender; drain.

Place remaining vegetable wedges and potatoes in ovenproof dish, sprinkle with wine, oil and herbs. Bake, covered, in moderately hot oven 40 minutes, remove leeks. Bake, uncovered, further 30 minutes or until vegetables are tender. Return leeks to dish, add celeriac, bake further 5 minutes or until heated through. Serve warm with garlic mayonnaise.

Garlic Mayonnaise: Process egg, yolk, mustard, juice and garlic until smooth, gradually add oil in thin stream while motor is operating, process until smooth, stir in chives.

Serves 4 to 6.

EGGPLANT WAFERS WITH YOGURT DRESSING

2 teaspoons sesame seeds
2 teaspoons sunflower seed kernels
½ teaspoon coriander seeds
1 teaspoon cumin seeds
1 large eggplant, thinly sliced
oil for deep-frying

YOGURT DRESSING
¾ cup (180ml) plain yogurt
1 clove garlic, crushed
½ teaspoon sugar
1½ tablespoons water
1½ tablespoons chopped fresh coriander

Place seeds on oven tray, toast in moderately hot oven about 5 minutes or until fragrant. Deep-fry eggplant in batches in hot oil until lightly browned; drain on absorbent paper. Place eggplant on plate; top with yogurt dressing, sprinkle with seeds.

Yogurt Dressing: Combine all ingredients in bowl; mix well.

Serves 4.

BROCCOLI AND EGG SALAD

700g broccoli, chopped
1 small red Spanish onion, sliced
6 green shallots, chopped
6 hard-boiled eggs, halved

DRESSING
¾ cup (180ml) mayonnaise
1 tablespoon lime juice
1 teaspoon seeded mustard
½ teaspoon French mustard

Boil, steam or microwave broccoli until just tender; drain, rinse under cold water, drain. Combine broccoli, onion and shallots in bowl, add dressing; mix gently. Top with eggs.
Dressing: Combine all ingredients in bowl; mix well.

Serves 4 to 6.

CRUNCHY PEA AND NUT SALAD

500g frozen peas
4 sticks celery, chopped
1 cup (150g) unsalted roasted peanuts
⅔ cup (100g) macadamias, toasted
**227g can water chestnuts,
    drained, chopped**

DRESSING
200ml creme fraiche
1 tablespoon light soy sauce
2 teaspoons sesame oil
¼ teaspoon honey
1 teaspoon lime juice
1 tablespoon chopped fresh parsley

Boil, steam or microwave peas until tender; drain, rinse under cold water, drain well. Combine peas, celery, nuts and water chestnuts in bowl, add dressing; mix well.
Dressing: Combine all ingredients in bowl; mix well.

Serves 6.

LEFT: From left: Eggplant Wafers with Yogurt Dressing, Winter Vegetables with Garlic Mayonnaise.
BELOW: From left: Broccoli and Egg Salad, Crunchy Pea and Nut Salad.

Left: Plates from Century Universe.

RED PEPPER, ONION AND TOMATO SALAD

2 medium red peppers
1 medium red Spanish onion, sliced
3 medium tomatoes, sliced

DRESSING
½ cup (125ml) olive oil
2 tablespoons red wine vinegar
1 clove garlic, crushed
1 tablespoon chopped fresh basil
1 tablespoon chopped fresh chives
½ teaspoon sugar

Quarter peppers, remove seeds and membranes. Grill peppers, skin side up, until skin blisters and blackens. Peel away skin, cut peppers into 1cm strips. Combine peppers, onion and tomatoes in bowl, add dressing; mix well. Cover, refrigerate 2 hours.

Dressing: Combine all ingredients in screw-top jar; shake well.

Serves 4 to 6.

BELOW: Clockwise from left: Parsley, Mint and Crisp Bread Salad, Cucumber and Asparagus Salad with Chillies, Red Pepper, Onion and Tomato Salad.
RIGHT: From left: Broccoli, Corn and Bok Choy Salad, Potato Salad with Sun-Dried Tomatoes.

Below: Cutlery, plates and bowl from Made Where.

CUCUMBER AND ASPARAGUS SALAD WITH CHILLIES

2 bunches (about 500g) fresh
  asparagus spears
4 small green cucumbers, seeded
1 tablespoon oil
2 cloves garlic, crushed
1 tablespoon chopped fresh lemon grass
¼ cup (60ml) water
2 teaspoons drained green
  peppercorns, crushed
2 teaspoons fish sauce
2 small fresh red chillies, sliced
¼ cup (60ml) lime juice
½ teaspoon sugar

Cut asparagus in half lengthways, then into 6cm lengths. Cut cucumbers into 6cm thin strips. Heat oil in pan, add asparagus, garlic and lemon grass, cook, stirring, until fragrant. Add water, peppercorns, sauce, chillies, juice and sugar, simmer, covered, about 2 minutes or until asparagus is just tender. Add cucumbers, stir until heated through.

Serves 4.

PARSLEY, MINT AND CRISP BREAD SALAD

2 Lebanese bread rounds
2 tablespoons olive oil
1 teaspoon dried basil leaves
2 cups firmly packed flat-leafed
  parsley, chopped
1 cup firmly packed fresh mint
  leaves, chopped
4 green shallots, chopped
3 medium tomatoes, chopped
1 small green cucumber,
  seeded, chopped

DRESSING
2 cloves garlic, crushed
¼ cup (60ml) lemon juice
½ cup (125ml) olive oil
1 teaspoon sugar

Split bread in half; brush split side of bread with oil, sprinkle with basil. Place bread rounds, split side up, on oven tray, bake in moderately hot oven about 5 minutes or until bread is browned and crisp; cool. Break bread into small pieces.

Combine bread, parsley, mint, shallots, tomatoes and cucumber in bowl, add dressing; mix well.
Dressing: Combine all ingredients in screw-top jar; shake well.

Serves 6.

BROCCOLI, CORN AND BOK CHOY SALAD

200g broccoli, chopped
1 bunch (about 350g) bok choy
1 cup (80g) bean sprouts
1 medium red pepper, thinly sliced
425g can young corn spears, drained
4 green shallots, sliced
¼ cup chopped fresh coriander

DRESSING
¼ cup (60ml) oil
2 tablespoons light soy sauce
½ teaspoon sesame oil
1 tablespoon grated fresh ginger
1 tablespoon lemon juice
1 clove garlic, crushed

Add broccoli to pan of boiling water, boil, uncovered, until just tender. Add bok choy to pan, return to boil, boil, uncovered, until bok choy is just softened; drain, rinse under cold water, drain. Combine broccoli and bok choy with remaining ingredients in bowl, add dressing; mix well.
Dressing: Combine all ingredients in screw-top jar; shake well.

Serves 4 to 6.

POTATO SALAD WITH SUN-DRIED TOMATOES

80g sliced pepperoni
1.2kg baby new potatoes, halved
⅔ cup (70g) drained sun-dried
  tomatoes, sliced
2 tablespoons pine nuts, toasted

BASIL MAYONNAISE
3 egg yolks
2 cloves garlic, crushed
2 tablespoons lemon juice
¾ cup (180ml) oil
½ cup firmly packed shredded
  fresh basil

Cut pepperoni into thin strips. Boil, steam or microwave potatoes until tender; drain; cool. Combine pepperoni, potatoes, tomatoes and basil mayonnaise in bowl; mix well, sprinkle with nuts.
Basil Mayonnaise: Beat egg yolks, garlic and juice in bowl until smooth. Gradually beat in oil a drop at a time, beating constantly until a little over a quarter of the oil is added. Pour in remaining oil in a thin stream, beating constantly; stir in basil.

Serves 6.

ASPARAGUS AND MUSTARD CRESS SALAD

1 bunch (about 250g) fresh
    asparagus spears
1 bunch (about 15) baby carrots
1 medium mignonette lettuce
250g mustard cress

MUSTARD DRESSING
1 tablespoon seeded mustard
1 teaspoon Dijon mustard
¼ cup (60ml) olive oil
2 tablespoons lime juice
½ teaspoon chopped fresh rosemary

Cut asparagus into 8cm lengths. Trim
tops from carrots. Boil, steam or
microwave asparagus and carrots until
just tender; drain, rinse under cold water,
drain. Combine asparagus, carrots, torn
lettuce leaves and cress in bowl, add
mustard dressing; mix gently.
Mustard Dressing: Combine all ingredients in screw-top jar; shake well.

Serves 4 to 6.

NUTTY BEAN SPROUTS WITH RED PEPPER

1 small iceberg lettuce
3 cups (about 240g) mung
    bean sprouts
1 medium red pepper, sliced
⅔ cup (100g) unsalted
    roasted cashews
1 tablespoon sesame seeds, toasted

DRESSING
2½ tablespoons light soy sauce
2 tablespoons lemon juice
½ cup (125ml) oil
½ teaspoon sambal oelek
1 teaspoon grated fresh ginger
1 clove garlic, crushed
½ teaspoon sesame oil

Combine torn lettuce leaves with remaining ingredients in bowl; top with dressing.
Dressing: Combine all ingredients in
screw-top jar; shake well.

Serves 6.

WARM PANCETTA AND WITLOF SALAD

150g pancetta
6 medium witlof
2 tablespoons olive oil
1 medium red Spanish onion, sliced
2 tablespoons chopped fresh parsley

Cut pancetta into 2cm strips. Cut witlof
crossways into 2cm lengths. Heat oil in
pan, add pancetta and onion, cook, stirring, until onion is soft. Add witlof, cook,
stirring, until witlof is just wilted. Add
parsley, serve immediately.

Serves 6.

PINK SALAD LEAVES WITH RASPBERRY DRESSING

4 large beetroot leaves
1 medium radicchio lettuce
1 medium red oak leaf lettuce
8 medium radishes, sliced
1 medium red Spanish onion,
    halved, sliced

RASPBERRY DRESSING
2 tablespoons raspberry vinegar
⅓ cup (80ml) oil
¼ cup (60ml) olive oil

Combine torn beetroot and lettuce leaves,
radishes and onion in bowl; drizzle with
raspberry dressing.
Raspberry Dressing: Combine all ingredients in screw-top jar; shake well.

Serves 6.

ROCKET, BASIL AND ONION SALAD

2 bunches (about 240g) rocket
½ small red Spanish onion,
    thinly sliced
1 cup firmly packed fresh purple
    basil leaves

DRESSING
2 tablespoons sherry vinegar
½ cup (125ml) olive oil
2 teaspoons horseradish cream
1 teaspoon sugar

Combine rocket, onion and basil in bowl;
drizzle with dressing.
Dressing: Combine all ingredients in
screw-top jar; shake well.

Serves 4.

*LEFT: From left: Nutty Bean Sprouts with
Red Pepper, Asparagus and Mustard Cress
Salad.*
*RIGHT: Clockwise from front: Pink Salad
Leaves with Raspberry Dressing, Warm
Pancetta and Witlof Salad, Rocket, Basil and
Onion Salad.*

Left: Plates from The Craft Centre.

TOMATO PARSLEY SALAD ON OLIVE CROUTES

4 thick slices rye bread
2 tablespoons olive oil
2 teaspoons olive paste
2 cups firmly packed fresh
    parsley sprigs
oil for deep-frying
2 medium tomatoes, sliced
150g mozzarella cheese, sliced
50g snow pea sprouts

DRESSING
¼ cup (60ml) olive oil
1 tablespoon sherry vinegar
1 clove garlic, crushed

Place bread on oven tray, brush with combined oil and paste. Toast in moderate oven until crisp. Deep-fry parsley in batches in hot oil until dark green and crisp; drain on absorbent paper. Top croutes with tomatoes, cheese, sprouts and parsley; drizzle with dressing.
Dressing: Combine all ingredients in screw-top jar; shake well.
Serves 4.

ABOVE: From left: Bitter Leaf Salad with Curry Yogurt Dressing, Peachy Leaf Salad with Dill Dressing.
LEFT: Tomato Parsley Salad on Olive Croutes.
RIGHT: Mixed Leaf and Flower Salad.

Above: White plates and spoons from Hale Imports; under-plates from Villeroy & Boch.
Left: China from Primex Products Pty Ltd.
Right: Bowl from Primex Products Pty Ltd.

BITTER LEAF SALAD WITH CURRY YOGURT DRESSING

2 medium witlof
1 bunch sorrel
2 medium radicchio lettuce
1 medium bunch curly endive

CURRY YOGURT DRESSING
½ cup (125ml) plain yogurt
½ teaspoon curry powder
1 teaspoon honey
2 tablespoons cream
1 tablespoon water

Cut large witlof leaves in half. Slice sorrel into thin strips. Combine witlof, torn lettuce and endive leaves in bowl; pour curry yogurt dressing over salad, sprinkle with sorrel.
Curry Yogurt Dressing: Combine all ingredients in bowl; mix well.

Serves 6.

PEACHY LEAF SALAD WITH DILL DRESSING

1 bunch (about 120g) rocket
2 medium radicchio lettuce
1¾ cups (about 60g) watercress sprouts
250g snow peas
2 medium peaches, sliced

DILL DRESSING
1 medium peach, peeled, chopped
⅓ cup (80ml) plain yogurt
1 tablespoon sour cream
1 teaspoon honey
1 tablespoon chopped fresh dill

Combine rocket, torn lettuce leaves, sprouts and peas in bowl, top with peaches and dill dressing.
Dill Dressing: Blend or process peach until smooth. Add remaining ingredients; blend until combined.

Serves 4 to 6.

MIXED LEAF AND FLOWER SALAD

We used unsprayed edible flower petals such as marigold, viola, strawberry blossom, lavender and nasturtium.

200g mixed baby salad leaves
¾ cup flower petals

DRESSING
1 tablespoon chopped fresh tarragon
1½ tablespoons champagne vinegar
½ teaspoon Dijon mustard
⅓ cup (80ml) macadamia oil
2 tablespoons olive oil

Combine leaves, petals and dressing in bowl; mix gently.
Dressing: Combine all ingredients in screw-top jar; shake well.

Serves 4.

BEST CAESAR SALAD

6 slices bread
oil for shallow-frying
1 medium cos lettuce
½ x 56g can anchovy fillets,
 drained, thinly sliced
1 cup (80g) grated or flaked
 parmesan cheese

DRESSING
1 egg
1 clove garlic, crushed
2 tablespoons lemon juice
½ teaspoon Dijon mustard
½ x 56g can anchovy fillets, drained
¾ cup (180ml) olive oil

Remove crusts from bread, cut bread into
1cm cubes. Shallow-fry cubes in hot oil
until browned and crisp; drain on absorbent paper. Combine torn lettuce leaves,
half the croutons, half the anchovies and
half the cheese in bowl, add half the
dressing; mix well. Sprinkle with remaining croutons, anchovies and cheese; top
with remaining dressing.
Dressing: Blend or process egg, garlic,
juice, mustard and anchovies until
smooth, pour in oil in thin stream while
motor is operating, blend until thick.
Serves 4.

ROCKET, WATERCRESS AND PEAR SALAD

2 bunches (about 240g) rocket
2 cups (about 100g) firmly packed
 watercress sprigs
⅓ cup (40g) chopped walnuts
 or pecans
1 large pear, sliced

DRESSING
3 canned pear halves
2 teaspoons red wine vinegar
¼ cup (60ml) walnut oil

Combine rocket, watercress, nuts and
pear in bowl; drizzle with dressing.
Dressing: Drain pears, reserve ⅓ cup
syrup. Blend or process pears, reserved
syrup, vinegar and oil until smooth; strain.
Serves 6.

*BELOW: From left: Best Caesar Salad,
Rocket, Watercress and Pear Salad.
RIGHT: Clockwise from top: Endive and
Daikon Salad with Red Pepper Oil, Warm
Spinach and Pepper Salad, Radicchio,
Fennel and Feta Salad.*

*Below: Glass bowl and oil bottle from Accoutrement;
tiles from Country Floors.
Right: Tiles from Country Floors.*

ENDIVE AND DAIKON SALAD WITH RED PEPPER OIL

1 medium (about 300g) daikon
½ medium bunch curly endive
1 small radicchio lettuce

RED PEPPER OIL
4 large red peppers
½ cup (125ml) olive oil

Peel and cut daikon into very thin
matchsticks. Combine daikon, endive and
torn lettuce leaves in bowl; drizzle with red
pepper oil.
Red Pepper Oil: Remove seeds and
membranes from peppers. Process peppers until well minced, push through fine
strainer into pan; discard pulp. Simmer
pepper juice, uncovered, until reduced to
⅓ cup. Combine pepper juice and oil in
bowl; mix well.
Serves 4 to 6.

RADICCHIO, FENNEL AND FETA SALAD

1 stick celery
½ medium fennel bulb, thinly sliced
1 medium radicchio lettuce
¼ cup (45g) small black olives
¼ cup (35g) pimiento-stuffed
 green olives
80g feta cheese, crumbled

DRESSING
⅓ cup (80ml) extra virgin olive oil
¼ cup (60ml) lemon juice
1 teaspoon fennel seeds, crushed
2 cloves garlic, thinly sliced

Reserve celery leaves, thinly slice celery.
Combine celery leaves, celery, fennel,
torn lettuce leaves and olives in bowl;
sprinkle with cheese, top with dressing.
Dressing: Combine all ingredients in
screw-top jar; shake well.
Serves 4.

WARM SPINACH AND PEPPER SALAD

1 medium yellow pepper
1 medium red pepper
1 bunch (about 650g) English spinach
1 small onion, sliced
½ cup (125ml) olive oil
1 clove garlic, crushed
½ teaspoon seasoned pepper
⅓ cup (80ml) balsamic vinegar

Quarter peppers, remove seeds and
membranes. Grill peppers, skin side up,
until skin blisters and blackens. Peel away
skin, cut peppers into strips. Coarsely
shred spinach. Combine peppers,
spinach and onion in bowl.
 Heat oil in pan, add garlic and
seasoned pepper, cook, stirring, 1 minute.
Add vinegar, stir until heated through. Add
dressing to salad; mix well.
Serves 4.

RED CABBAGE, WATERCRESS AND FETA SALAD

1 medium cos lettuce
¼ medium red cabbage,
    finely shredded
2 cups (about 100g) firmly packed
    watercress leaves
200g feta cheese, crumbled

DRESSING
1 clove garlic, crushed
1 teaspoon chopped fresh thyme
1½ teaspoons Dijon mustard
2 tablespoons red wine vinegar
½ cup (125ml) olive oil
¼ teaspoon sugar
¼ teaspoon cracked
    black peppercorns
¼ teaspoon paprika

Combine torn lettuce leaves, cabbage and watercress in bowl; sprinkle with cheese, drizzle with dressing.
Dressing: Combine all ingredients in screw-top jar; shake well.

Serves 4 to 6.

BEETROOT CRISP SALAD WITH CITRUS DRESSING

2 medium zucchini
oil for deep-frying
4 medium beetroot, peeled
½ teaspoon celery salt
1 small butter lettuce
1 small coral lettuce

CITRUS DRESSING
1 teaspoon grated lime rind
1 tablespoon lime juice
¼ cup (60ml) orange juice
¼ cup (60ml) oil
1 clove garlic, crushed
½ teaspoon sugar

Using vegetable peeler, peel zucchini lengthways to form thin ribbons. Deep-fry zucchini in batches in hot oil until lightly browned and crisp; drain on absorbent paper. Thinly slice beetroot, deep-fry in batches in hot oil until crisp; drain on absorbent paper. Sprinkle zucchini and beetroot crisps with celery salt.
    Combine torn lettuce leaves and citrus dressing in bowl, top with zucchini and beetroot crisps.
Citrus Dressing: Combine all ingredients in screw-top jar; shake well.

Serves 4 to 6.

SPINACH AND THREE SPROUTS SALAD

8 English spinach leaves, shredded
4 large butter lettuce
    leaves, shredded
1 small green cucumber,
    seeded, chopped
8 cherry tomatoes, halved
1 cup (80g) mung bean sprouts
1 cup (70g) lentil sprouts
1 cup (40g) alfalfa sprouts

DRESSING
¼ cup (60ml) tomato juice
1 tablespoon white wine vinegar
½ teaspoon sambal oelek
1 clove garlic, crushed
¼ cup (60ml) olive oil

Combine all ingredients in bowl, add dressing; mix well.
Dressing: Combine all ingredients in screw-top jar; shake well.

Serves 6.

SPINACH AND MACADAMIA SALAD

1 bunch (about 650g) English spinach
50g snow pea sprouts
¾ cup (125g) macadamias,
    halved, toasted
½ cup (75g) sliced dried apricots

DRESSING
⅓ cup (80ml) macadamia oil
1 tablespoon white wine vinegar
1 clove garlic, crushed
¼ teaspoon sugar

Tear spinach into pieces. Combine all ingredients in bowl, add dressing; mix well.
Dressing: Combine all ingredients in screw-top jar; shake well.

Serves 6.

ENDIVE, GOATS' CHEESE AND POMEGRANATE SALAD

1 medium pomegranate
1 small curly endive
1 small green oak leaf lettuce
150g goats' cheese, crumbled
2 tablespoons chopped fresh chives
2 tablespoons shredded fresh basil

DRESSING
2½ tablespoons sherry vinegar
1 clove garlic, crushed
½ cup (125ml) olive oil
¼ teaspoon cracked
    black peppercorns

Remove seeds from pomegranate, discard skin and pith. Combine endive and torn lettuce leaves in bowl, sprinkle with pomegranate seeds, cheese and herbs; drizzle with dressing.
Dressing: Combine all ingredients in screw-top jar; shake well.

Serves 4 to 6.

LEFT: Clockwise from back: Spinach and Three Sprouts Salad, Red Cabbage, Watercress and Feta Salad, Beetroot Crisp Salad with Citrus Dressing.
ABOVE: From left: Spinach and Macadamia Salad, Endive, Goats' Cheese and Pomegranate Salad.

Left: Tiles from Country Floors.
Above: Plates from Century Universe.

ORANGE, ONION AND OLIVE SALAD

1½ tablespoons olive oil
2 large onions, sliced
1½ teaspoons grated orange rind
2 tablespoons sugar
2 tablespoons white vinegar
⅓ cup (80ml) orange juice
1 cup (about 50g) firmly packed
   watercress sprigs
3 medium oranges, segmented
1 green shallot, finely chopped
2 tablespoons small black olives
3 teaspoons brown vinegar
1 tablespoon olive oil, extra

Heat oil in pan, add onions and rind, cook, covered, stirring occasionally, about 10 minutes or until onions are soft. Add sugar, white vinegar and juice, simmer, uncovered, about 30 minutes or until thick; cool.

   Combine onion mixture and watercress in bowl, top with oranges, shallot and olives. Drizzle with combined brown vinegar and extra oil.

Serves 4.

SPICED TROPICAL FRUIT SALAD

1 medium coconut
1 medium papaw, chopped
1 large mango, chopped
1 stick celery, finely chopped

SPICY COCONUT DRESSING
1 tablespoon chopped fresh chives
1 small fresh red chilli, sliced
2 tablespoons chopped
   fresh coriander
⅔ cup (160ml) coconut milk
2 tablespoons lime juice
3 teaspoons fish sauce
2 teaspoons grated fresh ginger
pinch ground saffron

Pierce holes in top end of coconut to extract liquid, discard liquid. Break open coconut, prise off outer shell, break flesh into pieces.

   Combine papaw, mango and celery in bowl; top with spicy coconut dressing. Serve with coconut.
Spicy Coconut Dressing: Combine all ingredients in bowl; mix until smooth.

Serves 4 to 6.

LEFT: From top: Spiced Tropical Fruit Salad, Apple and Date Salad, Orange, Onion and Olive Salad.
RIGHT: From top: Grapefruit and Spinach Salad, Fruity Spaghetti Salad.

Left: Large bowl by Velta Vilmanis for The Glass Artist's Gallery; small bowl by Sallie Portnoy for The Glass Artist's Gallery; spoon from Dinosaur Designs.

APPLE AND DATE SALAD

2 medium red apples
½ cup (80g) pitted dates
¼ cup (10g) flaked coconut, toasted

DRESSING
¼ cup (60ml) dry white wine
¼ cup (60ml) oil
¼ cup (60ml) cream
1 tablespoon lemon juice
2 teaspoons sugar
2 teaspoons honey
2 teaspoons dark rum

Cut apples into thin wedges. Cut dates into thin strips. Combine apples, dates, coconut and dressing in bowl; mix gently.
Dressing: Combine all ingredients in screw-top jar; shake well.

Serves 6.

FRUITY SPAGHETTI SALAD

1 small rockmelon
1 small pineapple
125g thin spaghetti pasta
250g jarlsberg cheese, cubed
1 cup (160g) almonds

MARINADE
1 tablespoon grated lime rind
⅓ cup (80ml) lime juice
2 teaspoons honey
1 tablespoon grated fresh ginger
1 teaspoon sugar

Cut rockmelon and pineapple into 2cm pieces. Combine fruit and marinade in bowl, cover, refrigerate 1 hour.
  Add pasta to large pan of boiling water, boil, uncovered, until just tender; drain, rinse under cold water, drain. Combine undrained fruit mixture, pasta, cheese and nuts in bowl; mix well.
Marinade: Combine all ingredients in bowl; mix well.

Serves 4 to 6.

GRAPEFRUIT AND SPINACH SALAD

½ bunch (about 320g) English
      spinach
2 medium grapefruit, segmented
¼ cup (20g) parmesan cheese flakes

DRESSING
2 tablespoons balsamic vinegar
2 teaspoons honey
⅓ cup (80ml) olive oil
½ teaspoon seasoned pepper
1 clove garlic, crushed

Top torn spinach leaves with grapefruit and cheese; drizzle with dressing.
Dressing: Combine all ingredients in screw-top jar; shake well.

Serves 4.

FIG AND GRAPE SALAD WITH PROSCIUTTO

4 slices prosciutto
2 bunches (about 240g) rocket
4 large figs, quartered
100g white grapes
100g black grapes
60g blue cheese

DRESSING
1 tablespoon sherry vinegar
2½ tablespoons olive oil

Slice prosciutto into thin strips. Place rocket leaves on plate, top with figs, grapes, prosciutto and crumbled cheese; drizzle with dressing.
Dressing: Combine vinegar and oil in screw-top jar; shake well.

Serves 4.

BELOW: From top: Fig and Grape Salad with Prosciutto, Avocado, Asparagus and Strawberry Salad.

Below: Plates by Velta Vilmanis for The Glass Artist's Gallery.

AVOCADO, ASPARAGUS AND STRAWBERRY SALAD

1 bunch (about 250g) fresh
  asparagus spears, chopped
1 medium red oak leaf lettuce
1 medium avocado, sliced
1 tablespoon pistachios

STRAWBERRY DRESSING
125g strawberries, chopped
1 tablespoon orange juice
2 tablespoons oil
1 teaspoon balsamic vinegar
¼ teaspoon freshly ground
  black pepper
½ teaspoon sugar

Boil, steam or microwave asparagus until just tender; drain, rinse under cold water, drain. Combine asparagus, torn lettuce leaves and avocado on plate; drizzle with strawberry dressing, sprinkle with nuts.
Strawberry Dressing: Blend or process strawberries and juice until smooth; strain. Combine strawberry puree with remaining ingredients in screw-top jar; shake well.
Serves 4.

PEAR AND APPLE SALAD WITH ROASTED CASHEWS

4 medium nashi pears, sliced
1 medium red apple, sliced
2 sticks celery, chopped
½ cup (80g) sultanas
½ cup (75g) unsalted roasted
  cashews

DRESSING
4 egg yolks
2 cloves garlic, crushed
2 tablespoons lemon juice
¼ cup (60ml) macadamia oil
½ cup (125ml) oil
2 tablespoons sour cream
2 teaspoons honey
2 teaspoons milk

Combine pears, apple, celery, sultanas and dressing in bowl; mix well, sprinkle with nuts.
Dressing: Blend or process egg yolks, garlic and juice until smooth. Gradually add oils in a thin stream while motor is operating, blend until thickened. Stir in cream, honey and milk; mix well.
Serves 6.

MELON AND BLUEBERRY SALAD

20g butter
½ teaspoon curry powder
1 teaspoon grated fresh ginger
½ cup (75g) chopped macadamias
1 stick celery, sliced
2 green shallots, sliced
½ medium (about 750g) rockmelon, sliced
100g fresh blueberries
¼ cup loosely packed watercress sprigs

DRESSING
⅓ cup (80ml) thickened cream
1½ tablespoons milk
1 tablespoon lemon juice
1 tablespoon chopped fresh parsley
½ teaspoon seeded mustard

Heat butter in pan, add curry powder, ginger and nuts, cook, stirring, until nuts are coated in curry mixture and lightly browned; cool. Combine nut mixture, celery, shallots, rockmelon and blueberries in bowl; drizzle with dressing and top with watercress.
Dressing: Combine all ingredients in bowl; mix well.
Serves 4.

GREEN PAPAW SALAD

10 (about 60g) snake beans
1 medium green papaw
⅓ cup (50g) unsalted roasted peanuts
2 tablespoons dried shrimp
1 clove garlic, crushed
1 small fresh green chilli, finely chopped
1 tablespoon palm sugar
2 tablespoons lime juice
1 teaspoon fish sauce
2 teaspoons chopped fresh coriander

Cut beans into 4cm lengths. Boil, steam or microwave beans until just tender; drain, rinse under cold water, drain. Peel and coarsely grate papaw. Blend or process peanuts, shrimp, garlic, chilli, sugar, juice and sauce until well combined. Combine beans, papaw and shrimp mixture in bowl; mix well, sprinkle with coriander.
Serves 4.

BELOW: From top: Green Papaw Salad, Melon and Blueberry Salad.

Below: Plates from Amy's Tableware; salad servers from Country Road Homewares; tiles from Pazotti.

PINEAPPLE, GRAPES AND BROCCOLI WITH CHEESE DIP

1 large pineapple
200g broccoli, chopped
200g black grapes

CHEESE DIP
½ cup (125ml) cottage cheese
¼ cup (60ml) plain yogurt
1 tablespoon fresh orange juice
1 tablespoon chopped fresh chives

Cut pineapple in half, remove and discard core. Cut into 5mm slices. Boil, steam or microwave broccoli until tender; drain, rinse under cold water, drain.

Serve pineapple, broccoli and grapes with cheese dip.
Cheese Dip: Combine all ingredients in bowl; mix well.

Serves 4.

ABOVE: From back: Pineapple, Grapes and Broccoli with Cheese Dip, Pear and Apple Salad with Roasted Cashews.

Above: Bowls and cutlery from Butler & Co.

BASIC SALADS & DRESSINGS

Prepared with care, the familiar, tried and true salads are always winners. Our favourite recipes featured here are quick to make, using readily available ingredients. They all serve 10, so there's plenty for entertaining at barbecues, buffets or banquets. However, if you're serving fewer people, the quantities can easily be adjusted without spoiling the flavour. It's also a boon to have a variety of basic dressings at your fingertips, ready to suit a variety of dishes and all tastes. Most dressings can be made a day ahead, but the salads are best made just before serving.

PASTA SALAD

500g pasta spirals
2 tablespoons olive oil
200g baby mushrooms, sliced
3 sticks celery, chopped
1 large red pepper, chopped
1 large green pepper, chopped
440g can corn kernels, drained
2 tablespoons chopped fresh parsley
1 cup (250ml) bottled Caesar
  salad dressing

Add pasta to pan of boiling water, boil, uncovered, until just tender; drain, rinse under cold water, drain. Combine pasta with remaining ingredients; mix well.
Serves 10.

GREEN SALAD

1½ medium iceberg lettuce
1 medium mignonette lettuce
2 sticks celery, chopped
1 medium green pepper, sliced
2 small green cucumbers, sliced
4 green shallots, chopped
1 medium avocado, sliced

DRESSING
2 tablespoons lemon juice
1 clove garlic, crushed
pinch sugar
½ teaspoon French mustard
½ cup (125ml) olive oil

Combine torn lettuce leaves with remaining ingredients in bowl, add dressing; mix well.
Dressing: Combine all ingredients in screw-top jar; shake well.
Serves 10.

TOMATO AND ONION SALAD

7 medium tomatoes, sliced
2 medium onions, sliced
⅔ cup shredded fresh basil
1 cup (250ml) bottled Italian dressing

Combine tomatoes and onions in bowl; sprinkle with basil, top with dressing.
Serves 10.

COLESLAW

½ medium cabbage, shredded
2 medium carrots, grated
1 medium red pepper, finely chopped
4 green shallots, finely chopped
1 cup (250ml) bottled coleslaw dressing

Combine all ingredients in bowl; mix well.
Serves 10.

LEFT: Clockwise from left: Pasta Salad, Green Salad, Tomato and Onion Salad.
ABOVE RIGHT: Clockwise from left: Rice Salad, Coleslaw, Bean Salad.

Left: China from Corso de Fiori; salad servers from Accoutrement.
Above right: Serving bowls from Interentre Imports.

RICE SALAD

2 cups (400g) long-grain rice
440g can corn kernels, drained
440g can pineapple pieces in
  natural juice, drained
1 medium red pepper, chopped
1 medium green pepper, chopped
1 cup (125g) cooked peas
4 green shallots, chopped
½ cup chopped fresh parsley
⅔ cup (160ml) bottled Italian dressing

Add rice to large pan of boiling water, boil, uncovered, until just tender; drain, rinse under cold water, drain. Combine rice with remaining ingredients in bowl; mix well.
Serves 10.

BEAN SALAD

310g can corn, lima beans
  and capsicum
310g can red kidney beans
2 x 450g cans three bean mix
2 x 310g cans chick peas
2 sticks celery, finely chopped
4 green shallots, finely chopped
⅓ cup chopped fresh parsley
¼ cup chopped fresh mint
⅔ cup (160ml) bottled
  French dressing

Rinse and drain canned corn mixture, beans and peas, combine with remaining ingredients in bowl; mix well.
Serves 10.

POTATO SALAD

2kg baby new potatoes, halved
DRESSING
1 cup (250ml) bottled mayonnaise
½ cup (125ml) bottled Italian dressing
½ cup (125ml) sour cream
6 green shallots, chopped
¼ cup chopped fresh chives
2 teaspoons French mustard
2 teaspoons sugar

Boil, steam or microwave potatoes until tender; drain, rinse under cold water, drain. Place potatoes in bowl, add dressing; mix well.
Dressing: Place all ingredients in bowl, whisk until combined.
Serves 10.

BEETROOT SALAD

3 x 825g cans sliced beetroot, drained
1¼ cups (310ml) sour cream
2 tablespoons prepared horseradish
¼ cup chopped fresh chives
1 tablespoon water

Rinse beetroot under cold water; drain well. Cut into 5mm strips. Combine sour cream, horseradish, chives and water in bowl, add beetroot; mix lightly to combine.
Serves 10.

BELOW: From back: Beetroot Salad, Potato Salad.

Front platter from Interentre Imports; salad servers from Accoutrement.

MAYONNAISE

We have given you a basic recipe for mayonnaise and 5 simple variations; each recipe makes about 1 cup.

BASIC MAYONNAISE

2 egg yolks
1 tablespoon lemon juice
½ teaspoon salt
½ teaspoon dry mustard
½ cup (125ml) olive oil
½ cup (125ml) oil
2 tablespoons milk, approximately

Blend or process egg yolks, juice, salt and mustard until smooth. Add combined oils gradually in thin stream while motor is operating; blend until thick. Spoon mayonnaise into bowl; whisk in enough milk to give desired consistency.

CURRIED MAYONNAISE

1 tablespoon curry powder

Add curry powder to dry pan, stir over heat until fragrant; cool. Blend curry powder with egg yolks, follow method for basic mayonnaise recipe.

HERB MAYONNAISE

2 tablespoons chopped fresh chives
2 tablespoons chopped fresh parsley
2 tablespoons chopped fresh basil

Follow method for basic mayonnaise; whisk herbs into completed mayonnaise.

LIME MAYONNAISE

2 teaspoons grated lime rind
1 tablespoon lime
**   juice, approximately**

Omit milk from basic recipe, whisk rind into completed mayonnaise, whisk in enough juice to give desired consistency and taste.

THOUSAND ISLAND MAYONNAISE

⅓ cup (80ml) tomato paste
⅓ cup (80ml) tomato sauce
1 tablespoon Worcestershire sauce
½ teaspoon tabasco sauce

Omit milk from basic recipe, whisk paste and sauces into completed mayonnaise.

GARLIC MAYONNAISE

3 cloves garlic, crushed

Blend or process garlic with egg yolks, follow method for basic mayonnaise.

ABOVE: Top row from left: Basic Mayonnaise, Lime Mayonnaise, Thousand Island Mayonnaise. Second row from left: Herb Mayonnaise, Curried Mayonnaise, Garlic Mayonnaise.

SALAD DRESSINGS

Here are 3 simple dressings to add zest and variety to salads. Each recipe makes about 1 cup.

FRENCH DRESSING

¼ cup (60ml) white vinegar
¾ cup (180ml) oil
½ teaspoon sugar
1 teaspoon French mustard

Combine all ingredients in screw-top jar; shake well.

ITALIAN DRESSING

2 tablespoons white vinegar
2 tablespoons lemon juice
½ teaspoon sugar
2 cloves garlic, crushed
¾ cup (180ml) olive oil
1 tablespoon chopped fresh basil
1 tablespoon chopped fresh oregano

Combine all ingredients in screw-top jar; shake well.

NUTTY DRESSING

¼ cup (60ml) lemon juice
1 tablespoon white vinegar
⅓ cup (80ml) oil
⅔ cup (160ml) walnut or hazelnut oil

Combine all ingredients in screw-top jar; shake well.

ABOVE: From left: French Dressing, Italian Dressing, Nutty Dressing.

Glass bottles from Accoutrement.

GLOSSARY

Here are some terms, names and alternatives to help

everyone understand and use our recipes perfectly.

ALCOHOL: is optional, but gives a particular flavour. Use fruit juice or water instead, if preferred, to make up the liquid content required.

ARTICHOKE HEARTS: available from supermarkets and delicatessens in bottles, cans and bulk.

BACON RASHERS: bacon slices.

BALMAIN BUGS: crustaceans; a type of crayfish.

BEANS, DRIED: adzuki, black-eyed, borlotti, broad, chick peas, red kidney, turtle (black kidney) – see below.

BLACK BEAN SAUCE: made from fermented whole and crushed soy beans, water and wheat flour.

BLACK BEANS, SALTED: fermented, salted soy beans. Canned and dried black beans can be substituted. Drain and rinse canned variety, soak and rinse dried variety. Leftover beans will keep for months in an airtight container in the refrigerator. Mash beans when cooking to release flavour.

BLUE SWIMMER CRABS: also known as sand crabs, Atlantic blue crabs.

BOK CHOY: Chinese chard. Use leaves and young, tender parts of stems.

BURGHUL: also known as cracked wheat, is wheat which has been cracked by boiling, then re-dried; mostly used in Middle Eastern cooking.

BUTTER: use salted or unsalted (also called sweet) butter; 125g is equal to 1 stick butter.

CAPERS: pickled buds of a Mediterranean shrub used as flavouring.

CELERIAC: tuberous root with brown skin, white flesh and a celery-like flavour – see below.

ABOVE: Celeriac.

CHICK PEAS: garbanzos.

CINNAMON STICK: dried inner bark of the shoots of the cinnamon tree.

COCONUT: desiccated coconut.

Cream: available in cans and cartons.

Flaked: flaked coconut flesh.

Milk: available in cans from supermarkets.

Shredded: thin strips of dried coconut.

CORIANDER: also known as cilantro and Chinese parsley, it is essential to many south-east Asian cuisines. Its seeds are the main ingredient of curry powder. A strongly flavoured herb, use it sparingly until accustomed to the unique flavour. Available fresh, ground and in seed form.

ABOVE: Clockwise from top: broad beans, borlotti beans, turtle (black kidney) beans, chick peas, red kidney beans, black-eyed beans. Centre: adzuki beans.

COUSCOUS: a fine cereal made from semolina.

CREAM: light pouring cream, also known as half 'n' half.

Sour: a thick commercially cultured soured cream.

Thickened (whipping): is specified when necessary in recipes. Double cream or cream with more than 35 percent fat can be substituted.

CREME FRAICHE: a mixture of sour cream with fresh cream; available in cartons.

CSABAI: a type of Hungarian salami, available from most delicatessens.

CURLY ENDIVE: a salad leaf, also known as chicory, pictured on page 124.

CURRY POWDER: a convenient combination of powdered spices. It consists of chilli, coriander, cumin, fennel, fenugreek and turmeric in varying proportions.

DAIKON: a basic food in Japan, it is also called the giant white radish.

DRIED SHRIMP: dried salted baby prawns.

EGGPLANT: aubergine.

FENNEL: has a slight aniseed taste when fresh, ground or in seed form. Fennel seeds are a component of curry powder.

FENNEL BULB: is eaten uncooked in salads or may be braised, steamed or stir-fried in savoury dishes.

FILLO PASTRY: tissue-thin pastry bought chilled or frozen.

FISH SAUCE: made from the liquid drained from salted, fermented anchovies. Has a strong smell and taste; use sparingly.

FIVE SPICE POWDER: a pungent mixture of ground spices which include cinnamon, cloves, fennel, star anise and Szechwan peppers.

FLOUR:

Plain: all-purpose.

Self-Raising: substitute plain (all-purpose) flour and baking powder in the proportions of 1 cup (150g) plain flour to 2 level teaspoons of baking powder. Sift together several times before using.

GARAM MASALA: often used in Indian cooking, this spice combines cardamom, cinnamon, cloves, coriander, cumin and nutmeg in varying proportions. Sometimes pepper is used to make a hot variation.

GHEE: a pure butter fat available in cans, it can be heated to high temperatures without burning because of the lack of salts and milk solids.

GHERKIN: cornichon.

GINGER:

Fresh, Green or Root Ginger: scrape away outside skin and grate, chop or slice ginger as required. To preserve fresh, peeled ginger, cover with dry sherry in a jar and refrigerate. It will keep for months.

GREEN PEPPERCORNS: available in cans or jars, pickled in brine.

GREEN SHALLOTS: also known as scallions and spring onions. Do not confuse with the small golden shallots.

HARISSA: sauce or paste made from dried red chillies, garlic, oil and sometimes caraway seeds.

HOI SIN SAUCE: a thick sweet Chinese barbecue sauce made from a mixture of salted black beans, onion and garlic.

HUMMUS: a paste of chick peas, tahini, garlic, lemon juice and olive oil.

JERUSALEM ARTICHOKE: a root vegetable resembling knobbly potatoes or root ginger – see below.

ABOVE: Jerusalem artichokes.

JUNIPER BERRIES: dried berries of an evergreen tree; they are the main flavouring ingredient in gin.

KONBU: kelp seaweed used in Japanese cooking – as an ingredient in dashi, to flavour rice for sushi, and also as a relish.

KUMARA: an orange-coloured sweet potato.

LAMB PROSCIUTTO: uncooked, unsmoked, cured lamb; ready to eat when bought.

LEMON GRASS: available from Asian food stores and needs to be bruised or chopped before using.

LENTILS: dried pulses. There are many different varieties, usually identified and named after their colour.

LETTUCE: more unusual varieties include butter, cos, coral, radicchio, green oak leaf, red oak leaf, pictured on page 124.

MIRIN: sweet rice wine used in Japanese cooking.

MIXED SPICE: blend of ground cinnamon, allspice and nutmeg.

MIZUNA: a green salad leaf, pictured on page 124.

NORI: a type of dried seaweed used in Japanese cooking as a flavouring, garnish or for sushi. Sold in thin sheets.

OIL: polyunsaturated vegetable oil.

Olive: virgin oil is obtained only from the pulp of high-grade fruit. Pure olive oil is pressed from the pulp and kernels of second-grade olives. Extra virgin olive oil is the purest quality virgin oil.

OKRA: a green, ridged, immature seed pod, also called lady's fingers – see below.

ABOVE: Okra.

OYSTER SAUCE: a rich brown sauce made from oysters cooked in salt and soy sauce, then thickened with starches.

PALM SUGAR: very fine sugar from the coconut palm. It is sold in cakes, also known as gula jawa, gula melaka and jaggery. Palm sugar can be substituted with brown or black sugar.

PAPAYA: also called papaw.

PAPPADAMS: made from lentils and sold in packages in different sizes.

PARSLEY, FLAT-LEAFED: also known as continental parsley or Italian parsley.

PASTRAMI: highly seasoned smoked beef ready to eat when bought.

PEPITAS: dried pumpkin seeds.

PEPPERS: capsicum or bell peppers.

PICKLED PINK GINGER: vinegared ginger in paper-thin shavings.

POLENTA: usually made from ground corn (maize); similar to cornmeal but coarser and darker in colour. One can be substituted for the other but results will be slightly different.

PRAWNS: also known as shrimp.

PROSCIUTTO: uncooked, unsmoked cured ham; ready to eat when bought.

PRUNES: whole dried plums.

PUMPKIN: we used several varieties; any type can be substituted for the other.

RICE VERMICELLI: rice noodles.

RIND: zest.

ROCKET: a green salad leaf, pictured on page 124.

ROCKMELON: cantaloupe.

SAFFRON: available in strands or ground form. The quality varies greatly.

SAMBAL OELEK (also ulek or olek): a paste made from chillies and salt.

SCALLOPS: we used the scallops with coral (roe) attached.

SEASONED PEPPER: a combination of black pepper, sugar and bell pepper.

SEMOLINA: the hard part of wheat which is sifted out and used mainly for making pasta.

SESAME OIL: made from roasted, crushed white sesame seeds. Do not use for frying.

SESAME SEEDS: there are 2 types, black and white; we used the white variety in this book.

SNOW PEAS: also known as mange tout (eat all).

SORREL: has broad, oval-shaped leaves with a bitter, slightly sour taste; pictured on page 124.

SOY SAUCE: made from fermented soy beans. The light sauce is generally used with white meat, and the darker variety with red meat. There is a multi-purpose salt-reduced sauce available, also Japanese soy sauce.

SPINACH (SILVERBEET): cook green leafy parts as required by recipes.

SPINACH, ENGLISH: a soft-leaved vegetable, more delicate in taste than silverbeet (spinach); young silverbeet can be substituted for English spinach.

STAR ANISE: the dried star-shaped fruit of an evergreen tree. It is used sparingly in Chinese cooking and has an aniseed flavour.

STOCK POWDER: 1 cup stock is the equivalent of 1 cup water plus 1 crumbled stock cube (or 1 teaspoon stock powder). If you prefer to make your own fresh stock, see recipes below.

SUGAR: we used coarse granulated table sugar, also known as crystal sugar, unless otherwise specified.

SUGAR SNAP PEAS: small pods with small, formed peas inside; they are eaten whole, cooked or uncooked.

SULTANAS: seedless white raisins.

SUNFLOWER SEED KERNELS: from dried husked sunflower seeds.

TABASCO SAUCE: made with vinegar, hot red peppers and salt; use sparingly.

TAHINI PASTE: made from crushed sesame seeds.

TERIYAKI SAUCE: based on the lighter Japanese soy sauce; contains sugar, spices and vinegar.

TOFU: made from boiled, crushed soy beans. We used firm tofu in this book. Buy it as fresh as possible; keep any leftover tofu in the refrigerator under water, which must be changed daily.

TOMATO:

Cherry Tomatoes: Tom Thumb tomatoes, small and round.

Paste: a concentrated tomato puree used in flavouring soups, stews, sauces, etc.

Sauce: tomato ketchup.

Sun-Dried Tomatoes: dried tomatoes, sometimes bottled in oil.

V8 VEGETABLE JUICE: available in cans and cartons.

WASABI PASTE: green horseradish.

WATERCRESS: has small, deep green, rounded leaves with a peppery flavour; pictured on page 124.

WINE: we used good-quality dry white and red wines.

WITLOF: also known as chicory or Belgian endive, pictured on page 124.

YEAST: allow 2 teaspoons (7g) dried yeast to each 15g compressed yeast if substituting one for the other.

ZUCCHINI: courgette.

MAKE YOUR OWN STOCK

BEEF STOCK

2kg meaty beef bones
2 onions
2 sticks celery, chopped
2 carrots, chopped
3 bay leaves
2 teaspoons black peppercorns
5 litres (20 cups) water
3 litres (12 cups) water, extra

Place bones and unpeeled chopped onions in baking dish. Bake, uncovered, in hot oven about 1 hour or until bones and onions are well browned. Transfer bones and onions to large pan, add celery, carrots, bay leaves, peppercorns and water, simmer, uncovered, 3 hours. Add extra water, simmer, uncovered, further 1 hour; strain.
Makes about 10 cups.
■ Stock can be made 4 days ahead.
■ Storage: Covered, in refrigerator.
■ Freeze: Suitable.
■ Microwave: Not suitable.

CHICKEN STOCK

2kg chicken bones
2 onions, chopped
2 sticks celery, chopped
2 carrots, chopped
3 bay leaves
2 teaspoons black peppercorns
5 litres (20 cups) water

Combine all ingredients in large pan, simmer, uncovered, 2 hours; strain.
Makes about 10 cups.
■ Stock can be made 4 days ahead.
■ Storage: Covered, in refrigerator.
■ Freeze: Suitable.
■ Microwave: Not suitable.

FISH STOCK

1½kg fish bones
3 litres (12 cups) water
1 onion, chopped
2 sticks celery, chopped
2 bay leaves
1 teaspoon black peppercorns

Combine all ingredients in large pan, simmer, uncovered, 20 minutes; strain.
Makes about 10 cups.
■ Stock can be made 4 days ahead.
■ Storage: Covered, in refrigerator.
■ Freeze: Suitable.
■ Microwave: Not suitable.

VEGETABLE STOCK

1 large carrot, chopped
1 large parsnip, chopped
2 onions, chopped
6 sticks celery, chopped
4 bay leaves
2 teaspoons black peppercorns
3 litres (12 cups) water

Combine all ingredients in large pan, simmer, uncovered, 1½ hours; strain.
Makes about 5 cups.
■ Stock can be made 4 days ahead.
■ Storage: Covered, in refrigerator.
■ Freeze: Suitable.
■ Microwave: Not suitable.

SORREL

BUTTER LETTUCE

MIZUNA

CURLY ENDIVE

CORAL LETTUCE

WATERCRESS

ROCKET

RADICCHIO LETTUCE

RED OAK LEAF LETTUCE

COS LETTUCE

GREEN OAK LEAF LETTUCE

WITLOF

INDEX

QUICK CONVERSION GUIDE

Wherever you live in the world, you can use our recipes with the help of our easy-to-follow conversions for all your cooking needs. These conversions are approximate only. The difference between the exact and approximate conversions of liquid and dry measures amounts to only a teaspoon or two, and will not make any noticeable difference to your cooking results.

MEASURING EQUIPMENT

The difference between measuring cups internationally is minimal within 2 or 3 teaspoons' difference. (For the record, 1 Australian metric measuring cup will hold approximately 250ml.) The most accurate way of measuring dry ingredients is to weigh them. When measuring liquids use a clear glass or plastic jug with metric markings.

If you would like metric measuring cups and spoons as used in our Test Kitchen, turn to page 128 for details and order coupon.

In this book we use metric measuring cups and spoons approved by Standards Australia.

● a graduated set of 4 cups for measuring dry ingredients; the sizes are marked on the cups.
● a graduated set of 4 spoons for measuring dry and liquid ingredients; the amounts are marked on the spoons.
● 1 TEASPOON: 5ml
● 1 TABLESPOON: 20ml

NOTE: NZ, CANADA, USA AND UK ALL USE 15ml TABLESPOONS.
ALL CUP AND SPOON MEASUREMENTS ARE LEVEL.

DRY MEASURES

METRIC	IMPERIAL
15g	½oz
30g	1oz
60g	2oz
90g	3oz
125g	4oz (¼lb)
155g	5oz
185g	6oz
220g	7oz
250g	8oz (½lb)
280g	9oz
315g	10oz
345g	11oz
375g	12oz (¾lb)
410g	13oz
440g	14oz
470g	15oz
500g	16oz (1lb)
750g	24oz (1½lb)
1kg	32oz (2lb)

LIQUID MEASURES

METRIC	IMPERIAL
30ml	1 fluid oz
60ml	2 fluid oz
100ml	3 fluid oz
125ml	4 fluid oz
150ml	5 fluid oz (¼ pint/1 gill)
190ml	6 fluid oz
250ml	8 fluid oz
300ml	10 fluid oz (½ pint)
500ml	16 fluid oz
600ml	20 fluid oz (1 pint)
1000ml (1 litre)	1¾ pints

WE USE LARGE EGGS WITH AN AVERAGE WEIGHT OF 60g

HELPFUL MEASURES

METRIC	IMPERIAL
3mm	⅛in
6mm	¼in
1cm	½in
2cm	¾in
2.5cm	1in
5cm	2in
6cm	2½in
8cm	3in
10cm	4in
13cm	5in
15cm	6in
18cm	7in
20cm	8in
23cm	9in
25cm	10in
28cm	11in
30cm	12in (1ft)

HOW TO MEASURE

When using the graduated metric measuring cups, it is important to shake the dry ingredients loosely into the required cup. Do not tap the cup on the bench, or pack the ingredients into the cup unless otherwise directed. Level top of cup with knife. When using graduated metric measuring spoons, level top of spoon with knife. When measuring liquids in the jug, place jug on flat surface, check for accuracy at eye level.

OVEN TEMPERATURES

These oven temperatures are only a guide; we've given you the lower degree of heat. Always check the manufacturer's manual.

	C° (Celsius)	F° (Fahrenheit)	Gas Mark
Very slow	120	250	1
Slow	150	300	2
Moderately slow	160	325	3
Moderate	180	350	4
Moderately hot	190	375	5
Hot	200	400	6
Very hot	230	450	7

TWO GREAT OFFERS FROM THE AWW HOME LIBRARY